Frequently Asked Questions on Corporate Japan

装幀 ● 菊地信義
装画 ● 野村俊夫

挿絵 ● 樋口太郎

Published by Kodansha International Ltd.,
17-14 Otowa 1-chome, Bunkyo-ku, Tokyo 112-8652.
No part of this publication may be reproduced
in any form or by any means without permission
in writing from the publisher.
Copyright © Yoneyama Morimasa and Richard Nathan.
All rights reserved. Printed in Japan.

First Edition 1998

98 99 00 01 10 9 8 7 6 5 4 3 2 1
ISBN4-700-2165-8

英語で話す日本ビジネスQ&A

ここが知りたい、日本のカイシャ

Frequently Asked Questions on Corporate Japan

米山司理 | リチャード・ネイサン

目次

CONTENTS

第**3**章　バブル崩壊と日本版ビッグバン　81

第**4**章　日本のおもしろ会社　111

CHAPTER **3** The Bursting of the Economic Bubble and Japan's Big Bang 81

CHAPTER **4** Exceptional Japanese Companies 111

CHAPTER 9 Recruitment and Employment in Japan 261

CHAPTER 10 Management and Ownership in Japan 289

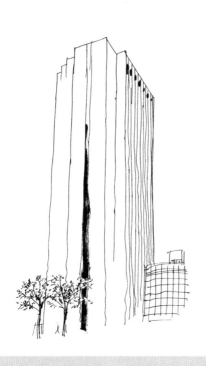

日本の会社あれこれ

Corporate Japan

・**1**

Question　**日本にはどれくらいの数の会社があり
ますか？**

Answer　株式会社が約80万社、有限会社が85万社、合
名会社と合資会社、相互会社が合わせて2万
7000社ほどあり、合計すると約168万社になり
ます。

　このうち株式を東京証券取引所の第1部もし
くは第2部に上場している会社が「大企業」と
いわれ、98年8月末現在で1819社あります。

　サントリーや竹中工務店、出光興産、朝日
新聞社、読売新聞社など株式を上場していな
い大企業や日本生命、第一生命など相互会社
の大企業もありますが、これらは例外で、ほ
とんどの大企業は株式会社で、しかも株式を
上場しています。

　上場企業に比べ規模がやや小さいのが、証
券会社の店頭で株式が取り引きされる「店頭
管理銘柄企業」です。855社あり、上場予備軍
とみられています。残り99％以上の会社は中
堅、中小企業です。

　中堅、中小企業は大企業の「下請け」や
「孫請け」、「曾孫請け」として大企業の製品の
部品を生産したり、一部業務を代行したりす

• 1

Q: How many companies are there in Japan?

A: There are about 800,000 joint-stock companies, 850,000 limited companies and 27,000 limited and unlimited partnerships, making a grand total of approximately 1,680,000 companies.

Of these, companies floated on the first and second sections of the Tokyo Stock Exchange are labeled major corporations. As of August 1998, there were 1,819 such companies. But a number of large, well-known Japanese companies are not floated on the stock exchange. These include Suntory Ltd., Takenaka Komuten Co., Ltd., Idemitsu Kosan Co., Ltd., Asahi Shimbun Publishing Co., the Yomiuri Shimbun as well as the mutual life insurance companies Nippon Life Insurance Co. and the Dai-ichi Mutual Life Insurance Co. They are, however, exceptional as the majority of large Japanese companies are joint-stock companies, whose shares are floated on the stock market.

The shares of over-the-counter stock companies, which are much smaller in scale than floated companies, are traded at retail outlets of security companies in Japan. There are 855 of these "up-and-coming companies" which are said to be preparing for future floatation. The remaining 99 percent of companies, which form the backbone of corporate Japan, are small and medium sized enterprises.

Many of these small and medium sized companies are either subcontractors or affiliated to large corporations. They manufacture product parts or carry out certain business activities

るところが多く、大企業1社に数百社、場合によっては数千社の中堅、中小企業がぶら下がっているのが日本経済の特徴です。

　当然、下請け企業の経営は、発注元の大企業の経営方針に大きく左右されます。独自の技術やノウハウを持って活動している中堅、中小企業もたくさんありますが、総じて日本は大企業中心の経済といえます。

・2

Question　**日本最大の会社はどこですか？**

Answer　売上高でみると商社が最も大きいのですが、商社の場合、仕入れが大きいと売上高も大きくなります。実際の収益は手数料なので、売上高は必ずしも会社の規模の目安にはなりません。

　商社を除くと、売上高が最も多いのはトヨタ自動車です。世界最大の自動車メーカー、ゼネラル・モーターズ（GM）の97年の売上高1781億ドル（約25兆円）には及びませんが、トヨタの97年度の連結売上高は11兆6783億円、当期利益は4543億円を計上しました。利益水準も日本一です。

　人口が約1000万人のギリシャの95年度の国

on behalf of major companies. Hundreds and, sometimes thousands of small and medium sized companies are suspended beneath large corporations forming intricate corporate structures, unique to the Japanese economy.

Management decisions at these subcontractors are, of course, strongly influenced by the business aims of the large companies from which they receive their orders. There are, however, also many active small and medium sized companies which have their own original technologies and know-how. Nevertheless, in general the Japanese economy is centered around large corporations.

• 2

Q: Which is Japan's largest company?

A: In Japan trading companies have the largest turnovers. But they purchase large quantities of goods on behalf of clients which boosts their overall turnover. In reality, they earn their profits through commissions and turnover is not necessarily a good criterion to measure corporate size.

Excluding trading companies, Toyota Motor Corp. has the largest turnover of all Japanese corporations. However, its turnover is not as large as General Motors Corp. (GM), the world's largest automobile manufacturer, which had a turnover of 178.1 billion dollars (25 trillion yen) in 1997. In 1997, Toyota's consolidated turnover was more than 11 trillion yen leading to profits of 454.3 billion yen. Toyota was also the number one company in Japan in terms of profitability. Greece, which has a population of some 10 million

内総生産（GDP）は約1100億ドル、当時の為替レートで計算すると約11兆円になります。トヨタの売上高はギリシャのGDP並みということになります。もっとも売上高とGDPを単純には比較できませんが。

　従業員数が最も多いのはNTTで約16万人です。民営化したばかりの85年には31万人いましたから、これでも半分近くに減ったことになります。NTTは15万人を目標にさらにスリム化を目指しています。ちなみにトヨタの従業員数は約7万1000人でNTTの半分以下です。

　ただ、NTTは99年には持ち株会社の下で、東西の地域会社などに分割されます。一方のトヨタはアメリカやヨーロッパにも工場を持つ世界企業で、海外の子会社を含めると従業員数はさらに膨らみます。総合的に考えるとトヨタが日本最大の企業と言えそうです。

・3

Question　**日本で最も古い会社はどこですか？**

Answer　日本で最初の株式会社は、明治政府が明治2年（1869年）に設立した「通商会社」と「為替会社」といわれています。現在、証券取引所に上場されている会社で最も古いのは、洋書が

people, had a gross domestic product (GDP) of about 110 billion dollars in 1995, or 11 trillion yen at the exchange rate at that time. Simple comparisons between turnover and GDP are not necessarily relevant but nevertheless Toyota's turnover and the total GDP of Greece are comparable in size.

However, the largest company in Japan in terms of the number of its employees is Nippon Telegraph and Telephone Corp. (NTT), Japan's leading telecommunications company, which employs 160,000 people. Shortly after its privatization in 1985, it had 310,000 employees. However, the number of employees has now fallen to about half that number and the company intends to reduce its work force to 150,000 in the future; whereas Toyota has a work force of 71,000, less than half that of NTT.

In 1999, NTT will be broken up into several companies including an east Japan regional company and a west Japan regional company within a new corporate structure managed by a holding company. Toyota, on the other hand, is a multinational corporation with offices and factories in the United States and Europe. When employees at its overseas subsidiaries are included, the total number of employees increases further. Overall, Toyota is Japan's largest company.

• 3

Q: Which are Japan's oldest companies?

A: Japan's first joint stock companies were the Commercial (tsusho) Company and the Exchange (Kawase) Company established in 1869 by the Meiji government. Currently, the oldest surviving company floated on the stock exchange is the

充実していることで有名な大手書店の丸善で、やはり明治2年の設立です。

　個人営業の商店は、創業から数えるともっと古い会社はあります。三井グループの創業は、江戸時代の延宝元年（1673年）にまで遡ります。この年に三井高利が江戸・日本橋に呉服を扱う越後屋を開きました。越後屋は大いに繁盛し、日本の代表的な百貨店の三越に発展しました。

　兼営していた三井両替店も江戸幕府の金銀御用達の地位を得るなど繁盛し、三井銀行となり、平成2年（1990年）には太陽神戸銀行と合併、その後、名称をさくら銀行に変更しました。さくら銀行は、三井グループの中核を占める都銀上位行です。

　住友グループの歴史も古く、元禄4年（1691年）に大阪の銅商「泉屋」が伊予（現在の愛媛県）の別子に銅山を開坑したのが始まりです。以来、銅の精錬、加工、販売へと事業を拡大、第二次世界大戦前には財閥となり、戦後も企業グループを形成しています。

　1996年に住友商事の社員がロンドン金属取引所（LME）を舞台にした銅取引に失敗、会社に約26億ドル（当時のレートで約2850億円）の損害を与えた事件がありましたが、住友グループはスタート時点から銅とは切っても切れない関係にあったのです。

major bookstore Maruzen Co., Ltd., famous for its range of foreign titles, which was set up in 1869.

However, if enterprises run by individuals and shops are included even older companies exist. The Mitsui Group was initially founded back in the Edo Period in 1673, the first year of Enpo, when Takatoshi Mitsui opened a fabric and drapery store in Nihonbashi in Edo, the former Tokyo. The store grew and prospered and developed into what is now probably Japan's most prestigious shop, the Mitsukoshi Department Store.

The Mitsui Exchange Shop, which was jointly managed by Mitsui, also flourished receiving the gold and silver business warranty from the Edo Shogunate (administration). Afterwards, it became the Mitsui Bank. In 1990, the bank merged with the Taiyo Kobe Bank Ltd. and changed its name to Sakura Bank. The bank occupies a central position within the Mitsui Group and is one of Japan's top city banks.

The Sumitomo Group also has a long history commencing in 1691 when the Osaka copper trader Izumiya opened a copper mine in Bessi, in Iyo, now Ehime Prefecture. Subsequently, it expanded its business into copper refining, processing and vending and finally transformed itself into a *zaibatsu* (conglomerate) before the start of the Second World War. After the war it continued operating as an industrial group of companies.

The Sumitomo Group has been involved in the copper business right from its inception, a relationship it has been unable to untie itself from. In 1996, a Sumitomo Corp. employee lost 2.6 billion dollars (285 billion yen at the exchange rate at that time) through a series of copper trades on the London Metals Exchange that went dramatically wrong. Luckily, the company had the financial resources to survive the loss.

• 4

Question 「財閥」とか「企業グループ」というのは何ですか？

Answer 持ち株会社を通じていくつかの大企業を支配している資本家一族のことを「財閥」と言います。

第二次世界大戦前は三井、三菱、住友、安田が4大財閥と呼ばれ、それ以外にも富士、日産などいくつかの財閥がありました。財閥はあまりに巨大になり、戦争遂行にも手を貸したため戦後、日本に進駐してきた連合軍総司令部（GHQ）は、「財閥こそ軍国主義の温床だ」として解体を指示しました。

連合軍が去って日本が独立すると、旧財閥系の企業などが再びグループを結成するようになりました。大きな企業グループは現在6つあり、旧財閥系は三菱、三井、住友の3グループ。銀行系が芙蓉、三和、一勧の3グループです。参加企業は互いに株式を持ち合い、ビジネス面でも協力し、戦後の高度成長の実現にも一役買いました。

グループ内の連絡や調整に当たるのは各社の社長が集まる社長会で、「金曜会」（三菱グループ）、「二木会」（三井グループ）などと呼ばれ、月に1回程度開かれています。

• 4

Q: **What are** *zaibatsu* **and industrial groups?**

A: The control of various large corporations by single capitalist families through stockholding companies are known as *zaibatsu*.

Before the Second World War there were four large *zaibatsu*, Mitsui, Mitsubishi, Sumitomo and Yasuda and various other *zaibatsu* including Fuji and Nissan. The *zaibatsu* grew to dominate the Japanese economy and as they were also incriminated in Japan's war effort, the General Headquarters (GHQ) of the Allied Powers in Japan dissolved them during the occupation of Japan, declaring that the *zaibatsu* were a hotbed of militarism.

After the Allied Forces left and Japan regained its independence the companies from the former *zaibatsu* began to reform into groups. There are now six large industrial groups in Japan, three based on the former *zaibatsu* Mitsubishi, Mitsui and Sumitomo. There are also banking groups including Fuyo, Sanwa and Ichikan. Companies within the same group own each other's stock and cooperate on the business front as well. They have been an important factor in Japan's rapid economic development since the war.

Communications and coordination within the groups are conducted by the presidents of each company at presidential meetings, such as the *Kinyokai* (Friday Meeting) of the Mitsubishi Group and the *Nimokukai* (Second Thursday Meeting) of the Mitsui Group, which take place approximately once a month.

　企業グループは、株式取得や役員派遣など
を通じ新たな企業を「系列」に取り込み、拡
大しようとします。こうしたグループ企業の
株式の持ち合いや系列取引は、1990年の日米
構造協議の際、日本市場の閉鎖性を象徴する
慣行として米国から槍玉に挙げられました。

　「大競争時代」の到来で、企業グループもも
たれ合い構造からの脱皮を迫られています。

・5

Question　**日本には持ち株会社はありますか？**

Answer　戦前の日本では財閥が持ち株会社を中心に企
業グループを形成していました。ところが戦
後、連合軍総司令部（GHQ）の指令により、
持ち株会社は禁止され、当時あった会社はす
べて解散させられました。
　アメリカやヨーロッパ諸国では持ち株会社
は禁止されていません。そこで独立後、経済
界は何回となく「国際競争で日本企業が不利
になる」と解禁を主張しましたが、実現しま
せんでした。

　バブル崩壊後の不況が長期化するにつれ、
「何かしなければ国際競争で生き残れない」と

Industrial groups expand their activities by pulling new companies into their *keiretsu* (group) and by acquiring shares or dispatching directors to companies. Cross shareholdings and the *keiretsu* structure of trading with companies within the group were targeted by the United States as one of the symbols of the closed state of Japan's markets to foreign businesses during the structural impediments initiative talks held by the United States and Japan in 1990.

However, as the era of mega-competition arrives these industrial groups are now being forced to compete openly and shed this structure of mutual reliance.

• 5

Q: Do holding companies exist in Japan?

A: In prewar Japan the *zaibatsu* formed industrial groups centered around holding companies. But after the end of the Second World War holding companies were banned by the General Headquarters (GHQ) of Allied Forces in Japan and all existing holding companies were dissolved.

However, in the United States and Europe, holding companies were and still are not prohibited. This led to numerous calls from Japanese business leaders, after Japan regained its independence, for the ban on holding companies to be lifted. The ban was said to be damaging Japanese industry's international competitiveness. Despite these calls the ban was not lifted.

The persistent period of economic stagnation in the 1990s following the bursting of Japan's economic bubble has awoken

の危機感が企業の間で高まりました。企業の要請に応じて公正取引委員会もついに重い腰を上げ、独占禁止法を改正、97年12月から50年ぶりに持ち株会社の設立が認められるようになりました。

　企業は一部の特殊なケースを除き、原則として自由に持ち株会社を設立できるようになり、ダイエーはさっそく、97年末に持ち株会社第1号として子会社40社を統括する「ダイエーホールディングコーポレーション」（DHC）を設立しました。

　NTTも99年夏には持ち株会社と長距離会社、東西の地域通信会社などに分割・再編される予定です。

　解禁はされましたが、持ち株会社と子会社の利益をならして法人税を納める連結納税制度が認められていないなど企業にとって魅力的でない部分もあり、多くの企業は設立に消極的です。

持ち株会社が認められない3つのケース

第1のケース　グループ資産が15兆円を超え、しかも5つの事業分野以上でそれぞれ総資産3000億円を超える会社を持つケース

第2のケース　総資産が15兆円を超える金融機関と総資産が3000億円を超える一般事業会社を持つケース

第3のケース　5事業分野以上（金融などは3分野以上）でそれぞれ有力会社（シェア10%以上または上位3位以内）を持つケース

a sense of crisis in Japanese industry. This has led to the fear that if radical changes are not implemented Japanese industry will no longer be able to survive global competition. These fears catalyzed the previously reluctant Fair Trade Commission to revise the Anti Monopoly Law in December 1997. After a gap of 50 years the establishment of holding companies was finally re-approved.

With the exception of certain special cases businesses were given the right, in principle, to freely set up holding companies. Daiei, Inc., moved quickly. At the end of 1997 it became the first Japanese company to set up a holding company, called Daiei Holdings Corp. (DHC), which unified 40 of its subsidiary companies.

In 1999, Nippon Telegraph and Telephone Corp. (NTT) plans to reorganize by splitting up into several companies including a holding company, a long distance telephone operator and two regional telephone companies covering the east and west areas of Japan.

Despite the ban on holding companies being lifted, a consolidated tax system, which allows the profits of holding companies and subsidiary companies to be evened out throughout the group of companies for corporate tax purposes, has not been approved. This makes the system relatively unattractive for companies and many companies have not actively taken up the opportunity to set up holding companies.

・6

Question	**日本にも国営企業はありますか？**
Answer	かつて通信事業や幹線鉄道は国営でした。経営は非効率でサービスも悪く、国民の評判はさんざんでした。このため日本電信電話公社（電電公社）は1985年に民営化されて日本電信電話（NTT）になり、タバコと塩を生産・販売する日本専売公社も同じ年に日本たばこ産業（JT）に衣替えしました。

87年には日本国有鉄道もJR東日本など7社に分割、民営化され、現在も残る最大の国営事業は郵便貯金です。

電電公社時代、通信事業は民間企業の参入が許されない独占体制で、日本の長距離通話料は世界で最も高いといわれました。民営化とともに新規参入が認められたため、新しいサービスが次々に登場、値下げ競争で料金も劇的に安くなりました。

鉄道も民営化でサービスは向上しました。国鉄は万年赤字で、穴埋めに税金をつぎ込んできましたが、JRになり赤字にもようやく歯止めがかかっています。

• 6

Q: Do state-owned enterprises exist in Japan?

A: Telecommunications and mainline railways were formerly run by the state in Japan. They were inefficient, provided poor services and had a terrible reputation. This led to the privatization in 1985 of Nippon Telegraph and Telephone Public Corp., which subsequently became Nippon Telegraph and Telephone Corp. (NTT). The state tobacco and salt manufacturing monopoly, the Japan Tobacco and Salt Public Corp., was also privatized in the same year becoming Japan Tobacco Inc. (JT).

In 1987, Japanese National Railways was split into seven separate companies including East Japan Railway Co. and privatized. Currently, the largest remaining state-owned enterprise is the Postal Savings.

When the state-owned monopoly Nippon Telegraph and Telephone Public Corp. still existed private companies were not allowed to compete with it in the telecommunications sector. At that time Japan had the highest long distance telephone charges in the world. Privatization allowed new participants to enter the market, which led to the introduction of a host of new services. A price cutting war developed which brought about dramatically lower telephone charges in Japan.

The privatization of the railways has also improved services. Japanese National Railways had been losing money for years and vast amounts of tax-payers' money were poured into this financial quagmire. But losses at the priva-

　96年、首相に就任した橋本龍太郎氏は行政改革を提唱、目玉は郵貯の民営化でしたが、郵政省とそれを応援する「郵政族」といわれる国会議員が猛烈な反対運動を展開したため、民営化は実現しませんでした。

　しかし、先進各国はいずれも小さな政府を目指しています。金融ビッグバンの中で、約240兆円に達する貯金を抱え、「世界最大の銀行」といわれる郵貯事業の民営化論議は今後も再浮上してきそうです。

• 7

Question　**日本企業の海外展開はどうなっていますか？**

Answer　日本は資源が少なく人口が多い島国で、海外から資源を輸入して加工し、製品を輸出する加工貿易を余儀なくされています。そのため開国後の明治時代から貿易に力を入れており、資源確保や製品販売などのため、企業は積極的に海外展開をしています。

tized Japan Railways (JR) are now showing signs of coming to an end.

In 1996, Ryutaro Hashimoto, a strong advocate for administrative reform, became prime minister. Privatizing Japan's Postal Savings system was one of his highest priorities. But the Ministry of Posts and Telecommunications and its supporting members of parliament, the so-called *yusei-zoku* (postal-tribe), objected fiercely and privatization plans came to nothing.

Advanced industrialized nations around the world are all trying to reduce the size of their governments and Japan is no exception. Japan's postal business which has more than 240 trillion yen of savings in its savings accounts is often referred to as the world's biggest bank. Privatization plans may not have led to anything this time but it is extremely likely that they will be reconsidered especially as Japan's Big Bang financial reforms progress.

• 7

Q: How are major Japanese corporations expanding overseas?

A: Japan is an island nation with limited natural resources and a large population. It is essential for its survival to be a trading nation importing natural resources from overseas and processing them into products for export. Since the opening of Japan and the Meiji Restoration, Japan has focused its efforts on international trade. Companies have expanded aggressively overseas in order to secure access to natural resources and markets for their products.

　特に1980年代以降は急激な円高の進行により、国内で生産していては輸出競争力を維持できなくなったため、自動車や電機など輸出関連企業が次々に生産拠点をアジアやアメリカ、ヨーロッパなどに移転しました。

　アジア諸国との間では生産品目を調整する水平分業が進んでおり、1997年から始まった通貨危機では日本企業も深刻な影響を受けました。

　工場進出だけでなく、バブル期にはジャパンマネーの力で日本企業は盛んに海外の企業や土地などを買い漁りました。ところが経営がうまくいかなかったり、土地が大幅に値下がりするなどその後、撤退する企業が相次いでいます。

　セゾングループは世界的な高級ホテルチェーンのインターコンチネンタル・ホテルを売却、松下電器産業もアメリカの映画会社、MCAの株を売却しました。

　銀行や証券会社もバブル期にはニューヨークやロンドンに一斉に進出、一時は国際金融市場で日本の金融機関のオーバープレゼンスが問題になるほどでしたが、バブル崩壊後は次々に撤退、信用度の落ちた日本の金融機関が海外でおカネを調達する場合、欧米の金融機関より高い金利を払わされるような状態にまで陥っています。

During the 1980s, following the sudden rapid appreciation in the value of the yen, it became impossible for domestic manufacturers to maintain their export competitiveness. One after another, automobile and electronic manufacturers with export orientated businesses moved their manufacturing bases to other Asian countries, the United States and Europe. This adjustment, a horizontal division of production, is shifting the manufacturing of various goods from Japan to countries across Asia. The currency crisis in the region, which began in 1997, is causing serious difficulties for Japanese companies active in the area.

In addition to the spread of Japanese factories overseas during the bubble economy, the strength of the Japanese currency encouraged many Japanese companies to buy up companies and land overseas. However, many companies later ran into financial difficulties and the price of land fell dramatically. This led to a subsequent rapid succession of companies withdrawing from their overseas investments.

The Saison Group bought the international luxury Inter-Continental Hotel Group and Matsushita Electric Industrial Co., Ltd. bought shares in the American film studio MCA. Both companies eventually pulled out, selling their investments.

During the economic bubble Japanese banks and security houses rushed to set up operations in New York and London and at one point the towering presence of Japanese financial firms in international markets caused great concern. But after the bubble economy collapsed company after company withdrew from these markets leading to a loss of confidence in Japanese financial institutions. Currently, when Japanese financial firms procure funds overseas they now find themselves in the situation of having to pay higher interest rates than American or European financial firms.

• 8

Question **会社はどういう形で倒産や破産するの でしょうか?**

Answer 「4大証券」の一角を占めていた山一証券が自 主廃業を決め、98年3月末で解散、約1万人の 社員は全員解雇されました。若手社員は引く 手あまたでしたが、中高年社員は再就職先が なかなか見つからず、会社がなくなる悲劇を あらためて見せつけました。

　山一は特殊なケースで、資金繰りが行き詰 まり、最終的に自主廃業という選択をせざる を得なかったわけで、倒産にはあたりません。

　日本で倒産というと、破産や特別精算、強制 和議、和議法上の和議、会社整理、会社更生手 続きという形で、会社を法律的に整理するケー スを指します。破産や特別精算は、事業を解散、 社員も全員解雇する精算型の倒産で、和議や会 社更正手続きなどは、債権・債務を整理して会 社を再建しようという方法です。うまくいけば 会社は再び生き返る可能性もあります。

　アメリカなど雇用が流動化している国と違い、 転職が難しい日本では倒産は社員にとって生 活の基盤を失いかねない深刻な事態です。こ

• 8

Q: How do Japanese companies go bankrupt or become insolvent?

A: Yamaichi Securities Co., Ltd., one of the "Big Four" security companies, decided to wind up voluntarily its business and dissolved in March 1998. Approximately 10,000 employees lost their jobs. Young employees were picked up by other financial firms but middle-aged and older employees found it difficult to find new jobs, highlighting the personal tragedy corporate failure brings about in Japan.

Yamaichi was in fact a special case. Its cash flow had dried up and it was finally left with only one option—to dissolve itself. But this would not normally be defined as bankruptcy in Japan.

In Japan bankruptcy is declared in cases where companies are legally liquidated through insolvency and special calculations, compulsory composition, composition based on the composition law, arrangement, and receivership. In the case of insolvency and special calculations the business is dissolved. All company employees lose their jobs and the company is liquidated and declared bankrupt. With arrangement and receivership, credits and debts are liquidated and the company is restructured. If all goes well it is possible for the company to be brought back to life.

Unlike in the United States and other countries with flexible and mobile labor markets, in Japan changing jobs is difficult. For employees in Japan bankruptcy is a very serious

のため経営者は倒産は何としても避けようとするのですが、不況期にはそうもいきません。

　民間の信用調査機関である帝国データバンクの集計によると、負債額が1000万円以上の97年の年間倒産件数は1万6365件、負債額の合計は14兆209億円と過去最悪を記録しました。クラウン・リーシングや東食などの大型倒産があったためですが、これには山一や北海道拓殖銀行の破綻は含まれていません。この2社を含めると実態はさらに悪いといえます。

　バブル崩壊のつけが一挙に押し寄せてきた感じで、倒産ラッシュはまだまだ続く可能性があります。

• 9

Question	**日本では合併・買収（M＆A）は盛んですか？**
Answer	ワールドコムがMCIを買収したり、トラベラーズ・グループがシティコープと合併するなどM＆Aが日常茶飯事のアメリカほどではありませんが、日本でも次第に増えています。 　日本の社員は会社への帰属意識が強く、合併しても社員のコミュニケーションがうまくいかないなどマイナス面もあり、経営者は合併には慎重でしたが、大競争時代を生き残るた

situation which results in them losing the basis for supporting themselves.

According to analysis by the private credit rating company, Teikoku Databank, in 1997 there were 16,365 cases of bankruptcies with debts of over 10 million yen and the total amount of unpayable outstanding debts reached an all time record of 14.209 trillion yen. This was partly due to the two large bankruptcies of Crown Leasing and Toshoku Ltd. But Yamaichi, which was not technically liquidated, and the failed Hokkaido Takushoku Bank are not included in these figures. If these two companies were included the actual figures would be even worse.

This sudden spate of corporate failures follows in the wake of the collapse of the bubble economy. This surge in the number of corporate bankruptcies is probably set to continue.

• 9

Q: Are mergers and acquisitions (M&A) common in Japan?

A: Mergers and acquisitions are beginning to increase in Japan but are not as common as they are in the United States where deals, such as WorldCom's bid for MCI and the merger of the Travelers Group with Citicorp, seem almost everyday occurrences.

Japanese employees feel a strong association to their companies, and one of the drawbacks with mergers in Japan is that even after a merger has been completed communications amongst the staff from the different companies do not

め背に腹は代えられなくなってきたようです。

　96年4月には三菱銀行と東京銀行が合併して世界最大規模の東京三菱銀行が誕生、10月には新王子製紙と本州製紙が合併して王子製紙になりました。97年10月には三井化学（三井石化と三井東圧化学が合併）、98年4月には吉富製薬（吉富製薬とミドリ十字が合併）と合併が相次ぎ、98年10月には秩父小野田と日本セメントが合併しました。

　バブル期には日本企業が海外企業を買収するケースが多かったのですが、バブル崩壊で様変わりし、採算の悪い海外事業の整理や縮小のため売却するケースが増えています。最近では、セゾングループが、88年に2800億円で買収したインターコンチネンタル・ホテルチェーンを約3700億円でイギリスの酒造大手のバス社に売却した例が話題になりました。

主な合併

92年12月	日本鉱業と共同石油	→ジャパンエナジー
93年 4月	十条製紙と山陽国策パルプ	→日本製紙
94年10月	小野田セメントと秩父セメント	→秩父小野田
10月	三菱化成と三菱油化	→三菱化学
96年 4月	三菱銀行と東京銀行	→東京三菱銀行
10月	新王子製紙と本州製紙	→王子製紙
97年10月	三井石化と三井東圧化学	→三井化学
98年 4月	吉富製薬とミドリ十字	→吉富製薬
10月	秩父小野田と日本セメント	→太平洋セメント

work well. Managers have taken a prudent attitude to date but to survive in the era of mega-competition mergers and acquisitions are now thought to be unavoidable.

In April 1996, the Mitsubishi Bank Ltd. and the Bank of Tokyo merged forming the world's largest bank, the Bank of Tokyo-Mitsubishi Ltd. A rapid succession of mergers is now beginning to take place in Japan. In October 1996, Shin Oji Paper Co., Ltd. merged with Honshu Paper Co., Ltd. forming Oji Paper Co., Ltd. In October 1997, Mitsui Chemical Inc. was formed with the merger of Mitsui Petrochemical Industries Ltd. and Mitsui Toatsu Chemicals Inc. and in April 1998, Yoshitomi Pharmaceutical Industries, Ltd. merged with the Green Cross Corp. Chichibu Onoda Cement Corp. and Nihon Cement Co., Ltd. also merged in October 1998.

During the bubble period there were many cases of Japanese companies acquiring companies overseas. But following the collapse of the bubble the situation changed. There are now more cases of Japanese companies disposing of their poorly performing overseas assets in order to restructure and reduce their overseas operations. A recent example is the Saison Group's sale of the Inter-Continental Hotel Group which it bought in 1988 for 280 billion yen, for 370 billion yen, to the large British brewer Bass.

・10

Question　企業の経営情報公開はどうなっていますか？

Answer　証券取引所に株式を上場している企業は、投資家に対し経営情報の公開（ディスクロージャー）が義務づけられています。

　合併や株主構成の大幅な変動など株価に大きな影響を与える経営情報はもちろん、毎年の決算内容も速やかに発表しなければなりません。インサイダー取引を防ぐため、公開の基準なども年々厳しくなっています。

　公開制度の中で大きな役割を果たしているのが、証券取引所内にある記者クラブです。企業は記者クラブで発表すれば、情報を公開したとみなされます。そのため東京証券取引所の記者クラブでは連日のように、さまざまな企業の経営内容についての発表が行われています。

　決算発表シーズンになると、狭いクラブ内は企業幹部や記者らでごった返します。日本の企業のほとんどは営業年度を1年としており、上場企業の約70％は4月1日から3月31日までを営業年度とする3月期決算です。

　取引所は決算終了後2ヵ月以内に内容を発表するよう指導していますので、例年5月の後半

• 10

Q: How do Japanese companies announce and disclose information about their businesses activities?

A: Companies whose shares are floated on the stock exchange are legally obliged to disclose corporate information to investors.

Information about mergers and significant changes in the composition of shareholders can substantially influence a company's share price and has to be made public quickly, in addition to the business information announced in annual company reports. To curb insider dealing, every year Japanese disclosure rules become more stringent.

Journalists based at the press room at the Tokyo Stock Exchange play an important role in publicizing Japanese corporate information. Companies make announcements to the media at the press room which they regard as publicly releasing information about their activities. Announcements from various companies about their business affairs are made everyday at the press room at the Tokyo Stock Exchange.

During the "results season" when most Japanese companies announce their annual results the small press room is packed with business executives and journalists. Most Japanese businesses have a 12 month financial year and 70 percent of floated companies in Japan keep to a financial year of 1 April to 31 March, which means most companies settle their annual accounts in March. Companies have to

には主要企業の決算発表が集中します。集中を避けるため記者クラブは、企業に対しできるだけ発表日を分散するよう要請していますが、あまり効果は上がっていません。

上場企業は、決算発表後にさらに詳細な経営情報を記載した有価証券報告書を大蔵省へ提出することも義務づけられています。

announce their results within two months of settling their year-end accounts. In an average year the announcement of results by the majority of Japanese companies is concentrated in the latter half of May. To escape this intense concentration during a short period, journalists have urged companies to lengthen the period when they announce their annual results. But these calls have met with little success.

In addition to releasing annual results, floated companies must also submit substantially more detailed information on their business activities in a printed securities report to the Ministry of Finance each year, after they have announced their annual results.

「30兆円産業のパチンコ」

日本ではルーレットやスロットマシンは禁止されており、カジノもありませんが、それに代わる手軽なギャンブルとして日本独特のゲーム「パチンコ」が盛んです。ピンボール台をタテにしたような機械上で、小さな鉄の玉をバネで弾き、穴に入れば玉がいっぱい出てきて、玉を景品に換えられるゲームです。

競馬や競輪、オートバイレースやボートレースなどの公営ギャンブルもありますが、パチンコはこうした公営ギャンブルをはるかに上回る日本で最大のギャンブル産業になっています。1995年のピーク時には全国のパチンコ店の年間売上高（貸し玉料ベース）は30兆円に達しました。

パチンコ店は中小企業や個人経営が多いのですが、なかには60を超える店舗を持ち、年間売上高が2500億円というパチンコチェーン店もあります。

パチンコの機械は、コンピューター制御のハイテク製品です。市場の拡大とともにパチンコ機メーカーも急成長し、トップ企業は90年代以降相次いで株式を上場しましたが、いずれも業績好調な優良企業です。

ただ、最近は「パチンコ依存症」が社会問題になったり、親がパチンコで遊んでいる間の幼児の事故続発などからイメージが悪くなり、客足は遠のき、売り上げは急減しています。プリペイドカードの変造事件や、勝ち負けの額が大きくなりがちな機械の導入も影響しているようで、不況知らずといわれたこの業界でも倒産する店が出ています。

Pachinko: A 30 trillion yen industry

In Japan roulette and one-armed bandits are banned and there are no casinos. But instead, for a quick and easy gamble, Japan has *pachinko*, a unique and thriving Japanese game. The game uses a machine which looks similar to a vertical pinball machine. Small iron balls are flicked with a spring-lever and if a ball enters a hole more balls come flooding out of the machine. These balls can be exchanged for prizes (including cash).

Publicly-managed gambling on horses, bicycles, and motor-cycles as well as motor-boats exists in Japan. But *pachinko* by far exceeds all publicly-run forms of gambling and is easily Japan's biggest gambling related industry. At its peak in 1995, the *pachinko* industry had an annual turnover of 30 trillion yen (in terms of ball rental). Most *pachinko* parlors are run by small or medium sized businesses or individuals. There are a few *pachinko* chains with more than 60 parlors and some with annual turnovers of up to 250 billion yen.

Pachinko machines themselves are high-technology computer controlled machines. The expansion of the *pachinko* market has created growth for *pachinko* machine manufacturers as well. From 1990, the leading companies were floated on the stock exchange one after another. Consistently good results have made them into blue-chip companies.

More recently, however, "*pachinko* addiction" has become a social problem. A series of fatal incidents involving children left alone while their parents played *pachinko* has damaged the industry's image, making it more difficult to attract customers. This has caused a sudden decrease in earnings. A scandal involving forged prepaid cards used for renting *pachinko* balls and the introduction of new machines with high loss to win ratios has also had a negative effect on the industry. Even in this industry, which was said never to experience recession, some bankruptcies are now occurring.

日本ビジネスのいま

Japanese
Business Today

・11

Question　**日本のベンチャー企業の現状は？**

Answer　マイクロソフトに代表されるハイテクベンチャー企業が続々と誕生、若い創業者が巨万の富を手にするアメリカのダイナミズムを見習おうと、日本でも官民挙げてベンチャー企業育成の試みがなされてきました。

　しかし結果は思わしくなく、ベンチャー企業はなかなか育ちません。理由は①ベンチャー企業に資金を援助する「エンジェル」（後援者）と呼ばれる投資家がほとんどいない　②ベンチャーキャピタルの数も資金量も少ない③アメリカの株式店頭市場（NASDAQ）に比べ、日本の店頭市場は沈滞していることなどが挙げられます。

　こうした環境面の遅れに加え、ハングリー精神を持った若者が日本には少ないことも一因ではないでしょうか。「寄らば大樹の陰」という発想で、日本の若者は大企業志向を強めています。

　それと日本の場合、ベンチャー企業といってもアメリカ流の圧倒的なハイテク技術を持った企業は非常に少数です。

• 11

Q: What is the state of venture businesses in Japan?

A: The seemingly endless creation of successful high-technology venture companies in the United States like Microsoft Corp. and the enormous wealth generated for their young founders as well as the current dynamism of the American economy, has attracted the attention of many people in Japan who wish to imitate these successes.

But local results have not lived up to expectations and successful venture businesses have proved to be very difficult to set up in Japan. Some of the reasons given for this are the small number of the so-called "corporate angels" and venture capitalists that supply financial support to venture businesses, and the inactivity of Japan's over-the-counter stock market relative to the market (NASDAQ) in the United States.

In addition to undeveloped conditions, a shortage of young people with the hunger and venture spirit needed to successfully start new enterprises may also be to blame. The idea that is encapsulated in the Japanese idiom "It is good sheltering under an old hedge" sums up the conservative attitude of many young people who rely totally on large companies to insure their livelihood.

Amongst the limited number of venture businesses in Japan very few follow the American model of being high-technology orientated. Moves are being made by government

　そこで一つの試みとして、大学の研究室が持っている特許や技術を生かしてベンチャー企業を興そうという動きがようやく始まりました。これまでは公務員の兼業禁止規定などさまざまな制約があり、実現しなかったのですが、これからはアメリカ型のハイテクベンチャーが誕生する可能性があります。起業家養成コースを設けるなど人材育成に乗り出す大学も増えています。

• 12

Question **日本企業のリスク管理はどうなっていますか？**

Answer 日本の企業や役所は、事故などに対する対応はマニュアルを作るなどしっかりしているのですが、国内の治安が良いせいか、警備や犯罪予防態勢ははっきりいってお粗末です。一部を除き企業や役所は犯罪には無防備の状態といえます。

　海外ではさすがにセキュリティーに力を入れていますが、それでも犯罪に慣れていないせいか警備は甘く、ペルーの日本大使公邸人質事件や三洋電機・メキシコ現地法人の社長誘拐事件など日本人が狙われる事件が相次いでいます。

　最近、企業にとって頭の痛い問題になって

bodies to encourage university research laboratories, which own patent rights and new technologies, to set up venture businesses. Until now, regulations that prevent civil servants, including university professors, from having second jobs have made this difficult; but the possibilities for creating American style high-technology venture businesses are now improving. The number of universities offering courses in business creation and personnel training is also growing.

• 12

Q: What type of risk management do Japanese companies conduct?

A: Japanese companies and government offices are excellent at producing manuals on how to deal with accidents but good public security and a high level of domestic law and order has led many Japanese private companies and public offices to take a lax attitude towards security and crime prevention. With the exception of a few companies and public offices most have no protection at all.

Outside Japan more effort is put into security but a lack of experience has led to extremely poor provision. The number of incidents targeting Japanese nationals, such as the hostage taking and subsequent siege at the Japanese ambassador's residence in Peru and the abduction of the president of a local Sanyo Electric Co., Ltd. factory in Mexico, is on the increase.

Recently another headache for Japanese companies is the

きたのは経営情報の漏洩です。97年10月には
NTT情報通信研究所のコンピューターネット
に何者かが侵入、業務データが流出する事件
がありました。98年には、さくら銀行の顧客
データが流出したり、高島屋の約50万人分の
顧客データが社員によって持ち出され、流出
する事件もありました。

　通産省の外郭団体、「コンピューター緊急対
応センター」の調査では、96年10月から97年
末までの1年3ヵ月間に企業などから寄せられ
たハッカーによる不正アクセスの報告や相談
は約500件ありました。この数字は氷山の一角
とみられ、日本の大企業や政府機関のコンピ
ューターシステムはハッカーたちの格好の標
的になっているようです。

　こうしたコンピューター犯罪から企業を守
るための支援をする企業も現れていますが、
経営者のセキュリティーに対する意識はまだ
低く、ハッカー天国はまだ続きそうです。

・13

Question　**企業の役員や職員による犯罪は起きま
すか？**

Answer　1997年は企業犯罪がつぎつぎに明るみに出た
記録的な年でした。総会屋に対し会社ぐるみ
で不正に資金を提供した野村や日興、大和、
山一の各証券会社と第一勧業銀行の幹部が逮

theft of valuable or sensitive corporate information. In October 1997, someone broke into the NTT Information System Research Laboratory's computer network removing confidential business information. In 1998, Sakura Bank's customer list was removed and an employee of Takashimaya Co., Ltd. walked off with data on 500,000 department store customers.

The Computer Emergency Response Center, an external organization affiliated to the Ministry of International Trade and Industry (MITI), received 500 reports and enquiries about unauthorized accesses to private company databases and networks by hackers between October 1996 and the end of 1997. These figures are probably just the tip of the iceberg. Computer systems belonging to the Japanese government and private companies are poorly protected and are quickly becoming the favored target for computer hackers.

Companies are now starting to appear in Japan which specialize in providing protection against computer crime. But awareness amongst management about computer security is still low and Japan is probably set to continue to be a hacker's paradise.

• 13

Q: Does white-collar crime exist in Japan?

A: 1997 was a record year for corporate crime in Japan with case after case coming to light. The illegal payment of funds to *sokaiya* (corporate extortionists) by many companies including Nomura Securities Co., Ltd., Nikko

捕され、松坂屋や三菱自動車工業などの幹部も総会屋への不正な利益提供で逮捕されました。

　総会屋は企業の不祥事などを調べ上げ、それをネタにおカネを要求、企業側も表ざたになって信用を失うのを恐れてカネを渡し、口をふさごうとします。

　社員による使い込み事件もありますが、最近はリスクの高い取引に手を出して会社に巨額の損失を与える事件が頻発しています。

　大和銀行ニューヨーク支店は95年、一人のトレーダーによる米国債の取引で約1100億円の損失を出し、結局、大和はアメリカからの撤退を余儀なくされました。

　翌96年には住友商事の非鉄金属部長が銅地金の不正取引で、大和事件を上回る約2850億円もの損失を出す事件が発覚、部長は詐欺罪の疑いなどで逮捕されました。

　イギリスでも「女王陛下の銀行」と呼ばれたベアリングズが95年、シンガポール支店のトレーダーが出した日本株の先物取引による約800億円の損失で事実上倒産に追い込まれました。相場で失敗するのは日本だけではないようです。

Securities Co., Ltd., Daiwa Securities Co., Ltd., Yamaichi Securities Co., Ltd. and the Dai-Ichi Kangyo Bank, Ltd. was uncovered. One executive after another was arrested from these companies. Matsuzakaya Co., Ltd. and Mitsubishi Motors Corp. executives were also arrested for granting illegal profits to other *sokaiya*.

Sokaiya dig into corporate scandals and use what they find to incriminate companies and demand cash. Companies, worried that if allegations are made public their reputations could be damaged, try to silence the allegations (by paying off the *sokaiya*). This type of corporate crime intertwined with *sokaiya* has been around for a long time in Japan and seems exceedingly difficult to put an end to.

There have been cases of embezzlement by employees but more recently incidents of employees losing vast amounts of their company's money, through risky deals, have occurred relatively frequently.

In 1995, at the New York branch of the Daiwa Bank, Ltd., one dealer single-handedly lost 110 billion yen on US government bond deals. Subsequently Daiwa Bank was forced to withdraw all its operations from the United States. The following year in 1996, Sumitomo Corp.'s nonferrous metals general manager lost even more with illegal copper trades which led to losses estimated at 285 billion yen. He was arrested on suspicion of fraud.

Japanese companies are not, however, the only ones to come a cropper in the markets. The British bank, Barings, which was nicknamed the "royal bank," went bankrupt in 1995, following losses of 80 billion yen run up by a rogue dealer trading future contracts in Japanese shares at the bank's Singapore branch.

• 14

Question | 日本企業の環境問題への取り組みは？

Answer | 1997年12月に開かれた温暖化防止京都会議で日本は、2008年から2012年の間までに二酸化炭素（CO_2）など温室効果ガスの排出量を90年よりも6%削減することを打ち出し、産業界は対応を迫られています。

自動車業界が取り組んでいるのは、モーターとガソリンエンジン併用の「ハイブリッド車」の開発で、トヨタは97年12月にハイブリッド車「プリウス」を発売しました。

トヨタは、将来のCO_2排出権取引市場の創設をにらみ、オーストラリアで植林事業にも乗り出しました。自動車工場などのCO_2削減が達成できない場合、取引の原資にしようという狙いがあるようです。

家電業界は家電製品の待機電力の削減に取り組んでいます。ソニーは、以前は5ワットだった大型テレビの待機電力を1ワットに削減しました。各社は製造工程での消費電力の削減も研究しています。

家電製品のリサイクル法も2001年には施行されます。当面の対象はテレビ、冷蔵庫、洗濯機、エアコンの4品目です。4品目だけで年

• 14

Q: How are Japanese companies dealing with environmental issues?

A: In December 1997, at the United Nations Kyoto conference on climate change, Japan hammered out an agreement to reduce carbon dioxide emissions and emissions of other greenhouse gases by 6 percent on 1990 levels between 2008 and 2012, forcing a response by Japanese industry.

The automobile industry is responding by developing a merged gasoline and electric motor hybrid car. In December 1997, Toyota Motor Corp. launched its Prius hybrid car. Toyota has also started planting trees in Australia in preparation for the establishment of a market for carbon dioxide emission trading. If it is unable to achieve reductions in carbon dioxide emissions at its factories it aims to use tree plantations as a resource to offset these emissions.

Japanese home electrical appliance manufacturers are improving efficiency by reducing the electrical charge used by appliances in a stand-by state before being switched on. Sony Corp. has already reduced the stand-by electrical charge in large televisions from 5 Watts to 1 Watt. Manufacturers are also currently researching how to reduce the amount of electricity consumed during the manufacturing processe.

The Recycling Law, for home electrical appliances will be enforced from 2001. Initially four types of products will be targeted—televisions, refrigerators, washing machines

間2000万台近く、重さにして約60万トンが廃棄されていますが、同法の施行により消費者は不要になった製品を処分する際、リサイクル費用と回収費用を負担しなければならなくなります。

　環境管理の国際規格である「ISO14001」の認証を取得する企業も急増しています。これまでは電機、機械などの大手メーカーが中心だったのですが、最近は建設や流通など非製造・サービス業や中小企業にも取得の動きが広がっています。

• **15**

Question | **日本企業の研究・開発への取り組みは？**

Answer | 日本のメーカーは、必死になって研究・開発に取り組んでいます。不況で利益は減っていますが、世界市場で闘うには先端技術開発で主導権を握ることが至上命題になっているからです。

　松下電器産業5000億円、トヨタ自動車4400億円、NEC3900億円、日立製作所3800億円など電機や自動車などは98年度も高水準の研究・開発投資を予定しています。キーワードはデジタルと環境です。

and air-conditioners. Every year 20 million units weighing approximately 600,000 tons of these four products alone are disposed of in Japan. Under this law consumers will have to pay for the cost of recycling and collecting unwanted products and goods.

The number of Japanese companies obtaining the international standard ISO14001 certification for environmental management is increasing. To date, this has been centered on large electronics and machine manufacturers but recently it has broadened to non-manufacturing companies such as construction and distribution companies, in addition to small and medium sized companies and service companies.

• 15

Q: How seriously do Japanese companies conduct research and development (R&D)?

A: Japanese manufacturers are fanatical about development. Despite the current recession and declining profits, developing cutting-edge technologies is still given the highest priority by manufacturers who wish to compete and lead in international markets.

Japanese electronics and automobile manufacturers plan to make high level investments in research and development in 1998. Matsushita Electric Industrial Co., Ltd. plans to spend 500 billion yen, Toyota Motor Corp., NEC Corp. and Hitachi, Ltd. plan to spend 440 billion yen, 390 billion yen, and 380 billion yen respectively. Current buzzwords are "digital" and "environmental" research.

　デジタルではテレビや画像、情報処理など
が各社の研究ターゲットです。半導体メモリ
ー（DRAM）開発競争もほとんどエンドレス
に続いています。現在、DRAMの中心は16メ
ガビットから64メガに移りつつありますが、
メーカーは2001年から2002年を目標に64メガ
の「次の次」の世代である1ギガや4ギガ
DRAMの開発を競っています。

　自動車各社が最も力を入れているのは、電
気自動車をはじめとする環境に配慮した車の
開発です。ＮＴＴはマルチメディア関連の技
術開発に重点を置いています。製薬各社は外
資の本格参入に備えて新薬開発に人とカネの
経営資源を思い切ってつぎ込んでいます。

　ただ、こうした努力にもかかわらず日本企
業は、情報通信やコンピューターのソフトウ
エア、バイオなど21世紀に基幹産業となる分
野の先端技術でアメリカ企業に後れをとって
いるのが実態です。

As far as digital related R&D is concerned the companies are targeting televisions, display technologies and information processing. Competitive development of semiconductor memory (DRAM) chips seems to continue endlessly. Currently, Japanese manufacturers are shifting their focus from 16-megabit to 64-megabit DRAMs. Manufacturers are already competing to develop between 2001 and 2002 the generation to replace the 64-megabit DRAM, the 1-gigabit DRAM and the subsequent generation after that, the 4-gigabit DRAM.

Automobile manufacturers are pouring their efforts into developing environmentally friendly automobiles starting with electrically powered cars. Nippon Telegraph and Telephone Corp. (NTT) is focusing on multimedia related technologies. Meanwhile, Japanese pharmaceutical companies are preparing for real foreign competition within the Japanese market by pouring management resources including funds and people into developing new drugs.

Nevertheless, the truth is that Japanese companies are behind American companies in information technology including computers and software as well as in biotechnology, which are expected to be core industries in the twenty-first century.

• 16

Question | **インターネットで企業はどのような影響を受けていますか？**

Answer | 最も大きいのは企業内の情報の共有化でしょう。社内の各種報告など電子メールを利用する企業が急増しています。

日産自動車の塙義一社長のように社員から来たメールに返事を出すトップも増えています。情報の共有化が進み、社内組織を見直すところも出てきました。

企業のホームページの開設は96年から97年にかけてブームになり、主要企業はほとんどがホームページを持っています。提供している情報は会社概要や採用情報、新商品紹介、プレスリリース、財務情報などで、経営のディスクロージャーや採用活動の手段として活用しているところが多いようです。

企業によってはマーケティングや通信販売の手段として利用しているところもあります。
今後、普及しそうなのは電子商取引（EC）です。すでに導入している企業もあり、導入企業は増えていきそうです。

• 16

Q: What effect is the internet having on Japanese companies?

A: The most significant effect the internet is having on corporate Japan is probably the increased sharing of information amongst staff within companies. The number of corporations using e-mail for internal company reports is increasing rapidly.

The number of top business executives, like Giichi Hanawa, the president of Nissan Motor Co., Ltd., who reply directly to e-mail they receive from members of their staff is also on the increase. The sharing of corporate information is even leading some companies to rethink their internal corporate structure.

Between 1996 and 1997 there was a boom in the number of companies launching homepages. Most leading Japanese companies now have homepages. They often contain information on the company's philosophy (or mission statement), recruitment information, information about new products, press releases and financial information. Many companies use their homepages to improve their openness to the public, to disclose business information and to enhance their recruitment activities. Other companies also utilize homepages for marketing and to conduct mail order business.

In the future electronic commerce (EC) is expected to increase in Japan. Some companies are already conducting electronic commerce but many more are expected to do so in the future.

朝日新聞、読売新聞など新聞社のホームページも充実してきています。新たな広告媒体として新聞社のホームページに注目するスポンサーもあり、ホームページ上に掲載される広告の取扱額も増えています。インターネット専門の広告代理店も登場しました。

日本でのインターネットの利用者は1000万人を突破しているとみられます。ネットワーク社会の到来で、企業経営は今後も大きな影響を受けそうです。

・**17**

Question 日本の会社の税制度はどうなっていますか？

Answer 企業の利益に対しては国税の法人税と、地方税である法人事業税、法人住民税が課され、事業年度が終了してから2ヵ月以内に申告して納税しなければなりません。

問題は税率ですが、はっきり言って国際的に見ても相当高く、産業界は「国際競争力の上で日本企業は不利」と不満たらたらです。こうした不満に応えるため、政府は98年度から法人税の税率を37.0%から2.5ポイント引き下げて34.5%にしました。この結果、地方税を含めて実際に企業に課される実効税率は46.36%になりましたが、それでもまだアメリカやイギリス、フランスなどに比べて高めです。

The homepages of the Asahi Shimbun Publishing Co. and the Yomiuri Shimbun, two of Japan's leading newspaper publishers, have become very substantial. Japanese companies are increasingly looking at the homepages of newspapers as a new advertising medium and overall income from advertisements on homepages is already on the rise.

The number of internet users in Japan is already said to have broken through the ten million barrier and the arrival of network companies is bound to have a huge effect on corporate management in Japan in the future.

• 17

Q: How does Japan's corporate tax system work?

A: Tax is levied on corporate profits nationally through corporation tax and locally through inhabitant tax and corporate enterprise tax. Companies in Japan have to declare their income and pay any tax due within two months following the end of the financial year.

But the most contentious issue in Japan is the rate of tax, which is extremely high by international standards. Japanese companies constantly grumble that these rates put them at a disadvantage in terms of international competitiveness. In response to these complaints the Japanese government decided in 1998 to reduce corporation tax rate by 2.5 points from 37.0 percent to 34.5 percent. Consequently, the total amount of tax actually levied on Japanese corporations including local taxes has fallen to 46.36 percent. This is still relatively high compared to many countries including the

　実は80年代初頭までは日本の法人税の税率は先進国の中でも低い方でした。それがその後、アメリカのレーガン政権やイギリスのサッチャー政権をはじめ多くの国が税率を引き下げたため、日本の税率が相対的に高くなってしまったのです。

　このため橋本龍太郎・前首相は、3年以内に法人税率を国際標準並みにするという方針を打ち出しました。小渕恵三首相もこの公約を引き継ぐとみられており、法人税は引き下げの方向にあります。

　企業は法人税以外にも営業内容によって固定資産税や消費税、印紙税、有価証券取引税などさまざまな税金を納めなければなりません。

・18

Question | **価格破壊とはどういう現象を指すのですか？**

Answer | 商品価格のこれまでの常識を「破壊」する大幅な安値販売をおこない、既存の店舗、企業から顧客を奪い取るのが価格破壊現象です。

　小売り業界で言えば、バブル崩壊後の1991年

United States, the United Kingdom and France.

At the beginning of the 1980s Japan's corporation tax was actually one of the lowest amongst industrialized nations. Subsequently, many countries followed the Reagan and Thatcher governments in the United States and the United Kingdom by cutting taxes, which left Japanese corporation tax relatively high by international standards.

Ryutaro Hashimoto, the former Japanese prime minister, announced when he was in office the intention of the government to reduce Japanese corporate tax rates to international levels within three years. Keizo Obuchi, the current Japanese prime minister, has stuck to this public pledge making it extremely likely that corporation tax will be reduced further.

In addition to corporation tax there are various other taxes related to business activities in Japan including property tax, consumption tax, stamp duty and securities transaction tax.

• 18

Q: What is price destruction?

A: The phenomenon of so-called "price destruction" is the poaching of existing customers from shops and companies through predatory pricing by selling products at much lower prices than they had previously been sold at, thereby destroying the standard established price structure of those products.

For example, following the collapse of the bubble economy

から94年ごろにかけて電機製品やお酒、日用品などのディスカウントストアが各地に誕生、安売りブーム、価格破壊が進行しました。円高で安い外国製品が大量に流入、規制緩和で店舗も増え、供給が増えたことが背景にあります。

小売店がメーカーと提携して従来の商品より大幅に安い普及品を開発、価格体系を壊す動きもあります。メーカー自身が価格の設定をやめ、小売店での価格は店が自由につける「オープン・プライス」も電機製品などを中心に増えています。

一時は景気の良かったディスカウントストアも最近は業績が悪化しています。それはスーパーや専門店なども軒並み価格を下げ、安売りがディスカウントストアの専売特許ではなくなったからです。小売業界の出店競争は続いており、供給過剰で値下がり傾向は今後も続きそうです。

サービス分野でも電話の通話料金は劇的に下がっています。これは価格破壊と言うよりむしろ、政府の規制で価格が割高に維持されてきたのが、規制緩和で正常な価格になったともいえます。

between 1991 and 1994, discount stores appeared across Japan selling electronic products, alcohol, and everyday goods at rock bottom prices. This discounting boom led to price destruction. The rising yen resulted in increased imports of cheap products from overseas. The easing of government regulations which made it easier to set up shops caused a proliferation in the number of discount stores across Japan.

Against this background of constantly increasing supply retailers developed successful new products which were much cheaper than those being supplied and marketed by existing manufacturers. This destroyed the existing pricing structures. Manufacturers have stopped fixing the retail prices for their products and increasingly allow retailers to set their own prices introducing a free pricing system. This has now become particularly common for electrical products.

The discount stores, which were initially very successful, have now fallen on harder times. Supermarkets and specialist stores have also started reducing prices and discounts are no longer the preserve of the discount store. Competition amongst shops in the retail industry is continuing and the oversupply of goods is causing a continuing downward trend of falling prices.

This is happening in the service industries as well. Telephone charges are also being cut drastically but this has more to do with the easing of government regulations, which had kept prices artificially high, than with price destruction per se. Telephone charges have now been reduced to relatively reasonable levels.

• 19

Question	**産業の空洞化現象とはどういうことで**
	すか?
Answer	円高の進行などにより、国内で生産していて

**産業の空洞化現象とはどういうことで
すか?**

円高の進行などにより、国内で生産していて
は国際競争力を維持できない産業が次々に工
場を海外に移し、その結果、国内産業が衰弱
する現象を、一般に「産業の空洞化」と言い
ます。

　アメリカでは1970年代以降、産業の空洞化
が進みましたが、日本では85年の「プラザ合
意」をきっかけにした超円高以降、急速に進
行しました。アメリカやヨーロッパの工場で
生産した車を輸入して国内で販売している自
動車メーカーや、日本国内には全く工場を持
たず、製品は100%海外の工場で生産している
家電メーカーもあります。

　海外で生産すれば人件費は国内の数分の一、
国によっては数十分の一になる場合もあるか
らです。製品によってはコスト面で事実上、日
本国内での生産が不可能なものも出ています。
　産業分野だけでなく、空洞化は金融分野で
も問題になっています。規制の残る日本の金
融市場を嫌い、日本の資金が海外に流出した
り、海外の金融機関が魅力のない東京市場か
ら撤退する動きもありました。東京証券取引

• 19

Q: Is deindustrialization taking place in Japan?

A: Domestic Japanese manufacturers who were unable to remain internationally competitive following the appreciation in the value of the yen during the 1980s, moved more and more of their factories overseas. This resulted in the weakening of Japan's domestic manufacturing base. This is generally described as the deindustrialization or hollowing out of industry in Japan.

Deindustrialization has continued in the United States since the 1970s. But the 1985 Plaza Accord, which triggered the rapid rise in the value of the yen, was the catalyst for a sudden progression of deindustrialization in Japan. Japanese automobile manufacturers now import cars from their factories in the United States and Europe and sell them in Japan. Japanese manufacturers such as electronics manufacturers who make 100 percent of their products overseas and do not have any factories in Japan have now come into existence.

Manufacturing overseas typically reduces labor costs to less than a tenth of those in Japan and in some countries the reduction can even be a hundred times or more. Some products, from the perspective of cost, are now impossible to manufacture in Japan.

This hollowing out is not just happening in manufacturing industries, it is becoming a problem for the financial sector as well. Lingering government regulation of Japan's financial markets is resented by the markets and has led to Japanese capital flowing overseas. Overseas financial institutions have

所に上場している外国企業も一時に比べかなり減りました。

しかし、ビッグバンの本格化で外国金融機関の目が再び東京市場に集まってきており、金融の空洞化にストップがかかる可能性もあります。ただ、そうなると今度は、東京市場の主力金融機関が外国系となり、国内金融機関は脇に追いやられる事態にもなりかねません。イギリスのウィンブルドン・テニス大会の主要プレーヤーが外国人選手となったような「ウィンブルドン化」が心配になってきます。

• 20

Question 日本の情報通信産業の未来は？

Answer パソコンや携帯電話、PHS、ファクス、電子交換機など情報ネットワーク関連機器の国内生産額は96年には17兆円を超え、初めて自動車の生産額（16兆円）を上回りました。

情報通信産業は世界的に急成長を続けてい

also started withdrawing from the Tokyo markets, which they view as unattractive and over regulated. The number of foreign companies whose shares are traded on the Tokyo Stock Exchange has dropped significantly.

However, Japan's Big Bang financial reforms have awakened a new interest from foreign financial institutions in the Tokyo markets, which may bring this hollowing out to a halt. But if this happens the main players in the Tokyo may end up being foreign financial institutions, with domestic Japanese companies only playing a minor role. This is causing concern about the so-called "Wimbledonization" of the markets, which would leave Tokyo in a similar position to Wimbledon in England. The internationally famous annual tennis tournament held at Wimbledon every year attracts players from all over the world but British tennis players only have a very minor impact at the tournament. Tokyo's financial markets are thought to face a similar fate.

• 20

Q: What future lies ahead for information technology related industries in Japan?

A: In 1996 domestic production of personal computers, cellular telephones, personal handy phones (PHS), electronic switching systems and various other communication network related products reached a value of more than 17 trillion yen. It surpassed the value of all automobile production in Japan for the first time ever, which remained flat at 16 trillion yen.

Communications systems and computer networks are

ますが、日本も例外ではなく、情報通信はいまや自動車に代わる基幹産業に育ちつつあります。

　日本で情報通信産業が注目されるようになったのは、国内通信の独占企業だった日本電信電話公社が民営化され、NTTになった85年以降です。電電公社の民営化とともに規制緩和で新しい通信会社が次々にでき、競争の結果、通話料は引き下げられ、携帯電話やPHSなどの移動電話も急速に普及しました。

　こうした通信分野のビッグバンとインターネットの民間への開放、パソコンの普及が相乗効果を発揮、急成長につながったのです。

　政府は2010年までに光ファイバー網の全国整備という目標を立てています。一方、放送分野でも2000年以降順次、地上波放送や衛星放送（BS）の方式はアナログからデジタルに移行する計画で、通信と放送の融合も進みそうです。

　通信、放送など情報通信産業の規模は2010年には120兆円に達するという予想もあります。この通り行くかどうかはわかりませんが、情報通信が21世紀の日本の基幹産業になることは間違いありません。

rapidly growing in number throughout the world and Japan is by no means an exception to this phenomenon. In Japan communications and information systems are now being nurtured as core strategic industries designed to replace automobile manufacturing in the future.

Telecommunications have been center stage in Japan since 1985 when Nippon Telegraph and Telephone Public Corp., which monopolized the domestic market, was privatized and became NTT. At the time of privatization regulations were eased and one new telecommunications company after another was set up. Increased competition led to falling prices and usage of mobile telephones including cellular and PHS telephones spread rapidly.

The big bang caused by this abrupt deregulation and the opening of the internet to the general public, as well as the increase in ownership of personal computers, created a synergy of demand which is closely connected to the rapid growth in this business area.

The government has announced plans to wire the whole of the country with fibre-optic cable by 2010. Meanwhile, in the field of broadcasting the plan is that from 2000 terrestrial and satellite broadcasting will switch from analog to digital systems which will further foster the fusion of the telecommunications and broadcasting industries.

It is predicted that these communications and information based industries will reach a total value of 120 trillion yen by 2010. No one can predict if development will really proceed in this manner but nevertheless there is no doubt that communications and information technology based industries will be core industries in Japan in the twenty-first century.

「企業内ベンチャーて何？」

企業が新規事業開拓のため社員から「起業家」を募り、資金を援助してベンチャービジネスを立ち上げる制度です。92年から93年にかけて大手企業の間でブームになりました。

アイデアを持つ社員に新規事業の計画を提案させ、社内の審査に合格すれば提案者が社長になり、事業を始めます。資金は会社と提案した社員の双方が出します。成功すれば提案者は社長としてそのまま事業を拡大、億万長者になることも夢ではありません。失敗したら元の会社に戻れます。

企業は、多角化のため新規分野を開拓したいが、なかなかうまくいかない。苦肉の策として思いついたのが企業内ベンチャー制度のようです。会社は資金を提供するわけですから成功すれば新規事業の開拓になるし、配当金も得られます。新規事業投資の新しい手法といえるでしょう。

ＮＥＣの社員が社内ベンチャー制度を利用して93年に設立した音響機器メーカーのオーセンティックは、高級スピーカーやパソコン用スピーカーなどで成功、95年度には早くも黒字になり、97年度の売上高は30億円を超えました。

しかし、オーセンティックは例外で、多くの社内ベンチャーは苦戦しており、すでに撤退した会社もあります。失敗しても元の会社に戻れるという身分保証が甘えを生んでいるという指摘もあります。

What is *kigyonai*-venture, intra-company venture business?

Kigyonai-venture is a system by which companies try to cultivate new businesses by recruiting existing employees as entrepreneurs and by providing financial assistance for the setting up of venture businesses. This boomed between 1992 and 1993 within major Japanese companies.

Employees with ideas were asked to draw up business plans. After an internal review if plans won approval the employee who had proposed the plan became president of the newly established company. Capital was put up jointly by both the company and the proposer. If the scheme was a success the proposer remained as president of the new company and through continued business expansion was given the real opportunity and not just the dream of becoming a multi-billionaire. On the other hand, if the venture failed the former employee was in principle allowed to return to his former company.

Japanese companies want to branch out and develop new areas of business but it is by no means easy. The internal venture business system was thought up as a last resort. Companies offer capital and if the venture is a success they can develop the business and obtain dividends. It can probably be described as a new investment technique for start-up businesses.

An NEC Corp. employee used his company's "intrapreneurialship program" in 1993 to set-up an audio maker called Authentic Ltd. which manufactures high quality speakers, and flat speakers for use in personal computers. In 1995, the company started making a profit and by 1997 its annual sales surpassed 3 billion yen.

Authentic is, however, exceptional. Most internal venture business programs turn out to be a battle against heavy odds and many companies have withdrawn their programs. Some people have also pointed out that the guarantee that you can return to the company if the enterprise fails is in principle fine but in fact may be rather optimistic.

バブル崩壊と日本版
ビッグバン

The Bursting of the
Economic Bubble and
Japan's Big Bang

• 21

Question 日本版ビッグバンは何を目指している
のですか？

Answer バブル崩壊と金融制度の自由化の遅れで地盤
沈下した東京市場をニューヨーク、ロンドン
並みの国際金融センターとして復活させるの
が最大の目的です。

　バブル全盛の80年代末期には、東京市場は
ニューヨークやロンドンと肩を並べる地位を
誇っていました。ところが、バブル崩壊とと
もに「護送船団方式」といわれる大蔵省の金
融行政の欠陥が明らかになり、がんじがらめ
の規制を嫌って資金は海外に流出するなど東
京市場の空洞化が進みました。

　市場が空洞化し、金融機関が国際競争力を
失ったままでは日本の経済は立ち直れないと
いう危機感から橋本龍太郎・前首相が96年秋
にぶち上げたのが、金融制度の抜本改革、す
なわちイギリスのビッグバンを見習った「日
本版ビッグバン」構想です。小渕恵三首相も
路線を継承、2001年の完全実施を目指してい
ます。

• 21

Q: What is the aim of the Japanese Big Bang financial reforms?

A: The collapse of Japan's bubble economy and delays in deregulation have damaged Tokyo's financial markets significantly. The main objective of the Big Bang is to restore Tokyo as an international financial center on a par with New York and London.

At the economic bubble's height, at the end of the 1980s, Tokyo's markets were proud to be ranked neck and neck with New York and London. But when the economic bubble burst systemic faults came to light within the Ministry of Finance's administration of Japan's financial system, through its so-called *gososendan-hoshiki* "convoy system" (which allowed all institutions to ride along equally as part of a group despite their relative financial strengths). Capital flight overseas also led to a hollowing out of the Tokyo markets, as investors became fed up with being bogged down by overbearing regulations.

In the fall of 1996, the continued hollowing out of the Tokyo markets created a sense of crisis reaching right up to Ryutaro Hashimoto, the prime minister at the time. The fear was that if financial firms remained internationally uncompetitive it would become practically impossible for the Japanese economy to recover. This was the catalyst for the plan to complete a series of radical reforms, mimicking the British "Big Bang" financial reforms of the 1980s under the grand concept of the Japanese Big Bang. Keizo Obuchi, the

　すでに銀行と証券会社との間の業務の垣根
は徐々に撤廃され、外国為替取引の自由化は
実現、金融持ち株会社の設立も認められるよ
うになりました。株式売買手数料も99年度末
までに完全に自由化される予定です。

　これまでなかなか実現しなかった改革を短
期間に一気に行おうという荒療治になります。
金融機関はバブルの後始末である不良債権処
理とビッグバンへの対応という2正面作戦を余
儀なくされています。

・**22**

Question | **約1200兆円といわれる個人資産の内容
は？**

Answer | 日本の個人金融資産は96年3月末で1183兆円、
国民1人当たりにすると約940万円になります。

　内訳は銀行預金が最も多く402兆円、郵便貯
金が213兆円あり、合わせると615兆円と資産
の半分以上を占めます。ほかは生命保険212兆
円、信託78兆円、株式46兆円、債券37兆円な
どとなっています。

current Japanese prime minister, has inherited the plans and intends to implement all the reforms by 2001.

Already partitions between banks and stockbrokers have been removed and foreign exchange trading has been liberalized. The establishment of financial holding companies has also been recognized. Commissions on the purchase and sale of stocks will be completely liberalized by 1999.

This series of financial reforms that had previously been proposed but had been difficult to implement will now take place all at once in a form of shock therapy in a short period of time. Japanese financial institutions now have to develop two-pronged strategies to deal with both the aftermath of the bubble economy and its associated bad loans, and the Big Bang financial reforms.

• 22

Q: What do the approximately 1,200 trillion yen of personally held assets in Japan consist of?

A: To be accurate the total amount of financial assets held by Japanese individuals as of March 1996 was 1,183 trillion yen, approximately 9,400,000 yen per person.

The largest proportion of these funds is held as bank deposits consisting of 402 trillion yen, followed by post office savings totalling 213 trillion yen. Combined this makes up 615 trillion yen or more than half the total amount of assets held by individuals in Japan. The remainder consists of life insurance policies worth 212 trillion yen, trusts worth 73 trillion yen, stocks worth 46 trillion yen and bonds worth 37 trillion yen.

　一方、アメリカの個人金融資産は18兆100億ドル、預金と貯金は合わせても全体の約16%にしかすぎません。その分アメリカ人は株式や債券に多額の投資をしています。

　これでわかるのは、日本人はアメリカ人に比べ資産運用に非常に慎重で、安全志向が高いということです。背景には国民性の違いがあるかもしれません。エコノミストらは、それに加えて金融の自由化の遅れで日本の銀行や証券会社がこれまで魅力的な金融商品を提供しなかったためだとみています。

　だからビッグバンをきっかけに銀行や証券会社が魅力的な金融商品を始めれば、個人資産の一部はそちらに動くはず、眠っていた1200兆円が動き出すとの思惑で、日本ではいま、内外の金融・証券会社が入り乱れて個人資産の獲得合戦が始まっています。

　たしかに5%が動いても60兆円、10%だと120兆円にもなります。生き残りをかけた金融・証券界の大競争は当分続きそうです。

However, in the United Sates individually held assets total 18 trillion 10 billion dollars, with deposits and savings combined only reaching about 16 percent of this total. This implies that Americans invest a much larger proportion of their savings in stocks and bonds than individuals in Japan do.

From these figures it is easy to grasp just how prudent Japanese people are compared with Americans in terms of investing money and the value they seem to attach to safety and security. There may be different cultural backgrounds at play, but economists argue that the real reason behind this difference in investment patterns is the delay in financial liberalization in Japan. The delay has stopped Japanese banks and security houses from creating and marketing attractive financial products in Japan.

If banks and stockbrokers can utilize the opportunity of the Big Bang financial reforms to introduce new attractive financial products, a significant proportion of personally held assets ought to move in their direction. With this in mind domestic and foreign financial firms are gearing up for the free-for-all battle to win access to the 1,200 trillion yen of dormant personal savings currently held in Japan.

If only 5 percent of these assets move it will be equivalent to 60 trillion yen; 10 percent will equal 120 trillion yen. Competition amongst financial firms, who are staking their survival on this, is set to continue for some time to come.

・**23**

Question｜**日本の金融機関の破綻はまだ続きますか？**

Answer｜97年秋には三洋証券、北海道拓殖銀行、山一証券、徳陽シティ銀行の経営が連鎖的に行き詰まり、破綻しました。山一は98年3月末で自主廃業し、会社更生法を申請した三洋も結局、再建はかなわず、清算という選択をせざるを得ませんでした。拓銀、徳陽も市場から姿を消しました。

　98年夏には日本長期信用銀行の経営危機が明らかになり、住友信託銀行が優良債権だけを引き取る形で救済合併することになりました。しかし、破綻は山を越えたとは言えず、まだ続きそうです。このため政府は、破綻を促進するための「ブリッジバンク」という制度の導入を決めました。

　ブリッジバンク制度では、破綻した銀行は政府が任命する「金融管理人」の管理下に置かれます。管理人は不良債権と優良債権を分けて不良債権は整理回収銀行（RCB）に移し、優良債権については借り手を保護するため融資を継続します。

• 23

Q: Are more Japanese financial institutions likely to go under?

A: In the fall of 1997, Sanyo Securities Co., Ltd., the Hokkaido Takushoku Bank, Ltd., Yamaichi Securities Co., Ltd. and Tokuyo City Bank, Ltd. all ran into difficulties and collapsed. At the end of March 1998, Yamaichi Securities Co., Ltd. voluntarily closed its businesses and Sanyo Securities which had applied for protection under the Corporate Rehabilitation Law failed to restructure its finances and was forced into liquidation. The Hokkaido Takushoku Bank, Ltd., and Tokuyo City Bank, Ltd., also disappeared from the markets.

In the summer of 1998, management problems facing the Long-Term Credit Bank of Japan, Ltd., also came to light. In an emergency rescue attempt the Sumitomo Trust & Banking Co., Ltd., offered to take over the bank just by taking on its performing loan book. However, it is too early to say if Japan is out of the woods in terms of corporate failures as more failures are still expected. In order to speed up this process and restore confidence in Japan's banking system the government has decided to introduce a "bridge bank" scheme.

Under the "bridge bank" scheme, failed banks will be managed under the umbrella of government appointed financial managers. Non-performing loans and performing loans will be split. Non-performing loans will be transferred to the Recovery Corporation Bank (RCB) and the performing loans will be continued in order to protect healthy borrowers.

　管理人は体力のある銀行と合併するか、債権を売却して清算するかの選択をします。この制度の導入によって不良債権や破綻処理が進むとみられます。

　金融関係者の間では、次に破綻しそうなところとして大手都市銀行や信託銀行、地方銀行などの名前が囁かれています。株価や地価が急速に持ち直せば別ですが、そうならない限り金融市場から退場を宣告される銀行はまだ出そうです。

・**24**

Question **金融機関の不良債権はどのくらいありますか？**

Answer 98年3月末時点の銀行や信用金庫など日本全国959の金融機関が抱える不良債権の総額は87兆5270億円に達しています。各金融機関は97年度中に売却などにより総額15兆円近い不良債権を処理したのですが、それでもまだこれだけ巨額の不良債権が残っているのです。
　不良債権の額が多いのは都市銀行、長期信用銀行、信託銀行の大手銀行19行で、総額は50兆2340億円、地方銀行は64行で15兆2470億円、第2地方銀行は63行で6兆3550億円です。残りの15兆6910億円は信用金庫や信用組合、農協などです。

The managers will then have to choose whether to merge the banks with healthy financial institutions or to liquidate them. The introduction of this system is expected to speed up the disposal of non-performing loans and faltering Japanese financial institutions.

Financiers are busy discussing which of various large city banks, trust banks and local banks they expect to be the next to go under. Unless land prices and stock prices suddenly recover, which seems unlikely, other banks are bound to announce their retirement from the financial markets.

• 24

Q: What is the extent of Japanese banks' bad debts?

A: The bad debts held by Japan's 959 financial firms including banks and credit associations reached a total of 87 trillion 527 billion yen in March 1998. Despite the disposal of almost 15 trillion yen of non-performing loans through sales and other activities by financial firms in 1997 this vast amount of bad debts remains.

The banks with large amounts of non-performing loans are the 19 city, trust and long-term credit banks. They have a total of 50 trillion 234 billion yen of non-performing loans. The 64 regional banks have a total of 15 trillion 247 billion yen of non-performing loans and the 63 second tier local banks have 6 trillion 355 billion of bad loans on their books. The remaining 15 trillion 691 billion yen of non-performing loans are held by credit associations and unions, and agricultural cooperatives.

　この不良債権は、貸出先を分類して「回収に重大な懸念がある債権」と「回収に支障を来す恐れがある債権」の合計です。必ずしも全部がこげついて回収不能になるわけではありません。一部には回収可能な債権も含まれているとみられますが、最悪の場合、回収できない可能性があります。

　しかも、これは各金融機関の自己査定によるものです。実態はもっと多く、地価の下落が止まっていないこともあり、総額は今もなお100兆円を上回るという見方もあります。

　日本政府は、金融機関の破綻処理の際に不良債権を買い取る原資などに総額30兆円の公的資金を用意していますが、これではとても足りそうもありません。

・**25**

Question　**郵便局は本当に世界最大の銀行ですか？**

Answer　その通りです。郵便局は全国津々浦々にあり、その数は約2万4600局。郵便業務が主体ですが、貯金も出来ます。

　日本の郵便制度はイギリスの制度を見習い、前島密によって明治4年（1871年）に導入されました。最初は郵便だけを扱っていましたが、4年後の1875年から貯金も扱うようになりました。

　そのころの東京には「宵越しの銭は持たな

Non-performing loans are split into different categories including "loans where there is great concern about their recoverability" and "loans where fears concerning problems associated with recoverability exist." These loans are not necessarily all unrecoverable—some recoverable loans are thought to be included amongst them—but in a worst-case scenario they may all be unrecoverable.

However, these figures are based on self-assessment by each financial organization. In reality the numbers are much higher. The fall in land prices has not yet come to an end and some people expect the real total of bad debts to have reached more than 100 trillion yen.

In order to dispose of faltering banks the Japanese government has pulled together 30 trillion yen of public funds to purchase non-performing loans from the banks but this does not look as if it will be sufficient.

• 25

Q: Is the Japanese post office really the world's largest bank?

A: Yes, it is. There are post offices all over the country totalling approximately 24,600. Mail is the main area of business but post offices can also collect savings.

The Japanese postal system is based on the British system. It was introduced in 1871 by Hisoka Maejima. Initially it only dealt with mail but 4 years after it was founded in 1875 it was allowed to start collecting savings.

At that time in Tokyo many people suffered from the so-

い」という「江戸気質」の人が多かったようで、貯金は集まらず、当時の政府は公務員にボーナスの一部を強制的に預けさせたりしたようです。

　第二次世界大戦後は日本人の貯蓄意欲が強くなり、貯金はどんどん増え、残高は98年3月末で約240兆円、民間銀行としては世界最大の預金量を誇る東京三菱銀行の4倍以上に膨らみました。

　郵便局は簡易生命保険（簡保）も扱っており、契約保険金額は206兆円。世界最大の銀行であると同時に世界最大の保険会社でもあります。イギリスやドイツ、フランスの郵便局も貯金を扱っていますが、イギリスの貯金残高は約8兆円、日本の郵貯がいかに巨大かがわかります。

　日本の銀行などは郵貯の民営化を主張していますが、郵政省は絶対反対の立場で、民営化はなかなか実現しません。

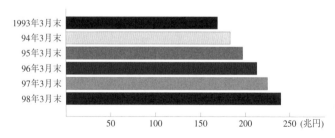

郵便貯金残高

1993年3月末	
94年3月末	
95年3月末	
96年3月末	
97年3月末	
98年3月末	

　　　50　　100　　150　　200　　250 (兆円)

called "Edo temperament" of not holding on to their earnings for more than one night and the post office found it very difficult to collect savings. To counter this, the government at the time made it compulsory for part of the bonuses paid to public servants to be paid into savings accounts.

After the end of the Second World War people became more conscious about the importance of having savings and the amount of savings steadily increased reaching today's level of 240 trillion yen. This has swelled to four times the total amount of funds held by the world's largest private bank, the Bank of Tokyo-Mitsubishi Ltd.

The post office also runs the Postal Life Insurance (*Kanpo*) which is worth 206 trillion yen making Japan's post office not only the world's biggest bank but also the world's largest insurance company. The British and German post offices also run savings accounts but the total amount of funds held by the British post office is approximately 8 trillion yen, which highlights the vast size of Japan's Postal Savings.

Japanese banks are calling for Postal Savings to be privatized so they can compete on a level playing field for the nation's savings. But the Ministry of Posts and Telecommunications strongly opposes this which makes privatization difficult.

• **26**

Question｜**農協は金融機関ですか？**

Answer｜農業協同組合（農協＝ＪＡ）は、1947年に制定された農業協同組合法に基づき、全国各地に設立された農家の相互扶助組織で、現在、約900万人の農業従事者が加盟しています。

　農機具や肥料などの農家への販売や農作物の集荷、販売を中心とする経済事業や組合員を対象とした金融、保険事業を営んでおり、国の手厚い農業保護策の恩恵を受けて事業規模は急拡大しました。全国の農協の貯金残高は98年3月末で68兆円を超えており、巨大な金融機関でもあります。

　普通の金融機関と違うのは、お金を運用する力が極端に弱いことです。審査能力が弱く、バブル期には住宅金融専門会社に巨額の資金を融資し、多額の不良債権を抱え込んでしまいました。

　バブル以前は金融、保険事業は黒字で、その黒字が経済事業の赤字を補ってきたのですが、バブル後、経営内容は急速に悪化しています。

• **26**

Q: Are Japan's agricultural cooperatives banks?

A: Japan Agricultural Cooperatives (JA) was established in 1947, as part of the Japan Agricultural Cooperatives Law. Subsequently, farmers in all regions of Japan set up self-help organizations which currently have about 9 million members all working within agricultural related businesses.

The cooperatives' main business activities are selling farming equipment, fertilizer and other items to farmers and collecting and selling crops and farm produce. In addition to this the cooperatives provide financial services and insurance to their members. Benefiting from the government's deliberate policy of protecting domestic agricultural related industries the cooperatives have quickly developed and expanded the scale of their operations. The total amount of funds held by all the country's agricultural cooperatives in March 1998 surpassed 68 trillion yen, making them a major financial institution.

However, the biggest difference between them and normal financial institutions is that cooperatives are extremely poor at making and assessing investment possibilities. Weak assessment capabilities led to the allocation of enormous loans to specialist mortgage companies during the economic bubble which eventually left the cooperatives holding large amounts of bad debts.

Before the economic bubble the financial services and insurance side of their business was profitable and helped cover losses on other business activities. But after the eco-

　このため全国各地の農協の合併を進めるとともに、現在「農協－都道府県の信用農業協同組合連合会（信連）－農林中金」という3段階の機構を「農協－農林中金」という2段階に簡素化して、効率化を図ろうとしています。

　しかし、農協は政府の補助金の窓口でもあり、保守系国会議員と結びついた政治依存体質から抜けきれず、自浄作用はあまり期待できません。経営の建て直しは難しいとみられます。

・**27**

Question **日本の株式市場は再生しますか？**

Answer 東京株式市場の平均株価は、1989年12月末に史上最高値の3万8915円87銭をつけましたが、バブル崩壊と景気後退で、その後かれこれ9年近くも低迷状態が続いています。

　バブル崩壊による株式下落で大きな損をした企業や個人投資家は、株式投資から手を引きました。これまで付き合いで取引先の株を持っていた銀行や企業も、業績悪化の穴埋め

nomic bubble burst their businesses rapidly deteriorated.

This has led to many mergers between agricultural cooperatives throughout the country. The three structural levels of the system which included Japan Agricultural Cooperatives, Prefectural Confederation of Agricultural Cooperative Trusts, and the Central Cooperative Bank for Agriculture and Forestry (Norin Chukin), have been simplified into two levels leaving Japan Agricultural Cooperatives and the Central Cooperative Bank for Agriculture and Forestry, in an effort to improve efficiency.

However, these cooperatives still act as liaison organizations for political funding and are closely tied to conservative members of parliament. They cannot seem to break the habit of relying on political support to boost their activities and also seem unlikely to be able to clean up their own organizations or rebuild their finances.

• 27

Q: Will Japan's stock markets recover?

A: At the end of December 1989 the Tokyo Stock Market's Nikkei average reached a record high of 38,915.87 yen, but the bubble economy then collapsed and a recession started. For almost 9 years since then stocks have continued to drag along at low levels.

Companies and individual investors, who were hit with large losses when the economic bubble burst and share prices fell, have retreated from the markets. Companies and banks who held shares in companies that they had business

のため株式を手放しています。

　国内に有利な投資先がないので企業の資金が海外に流出していることも株価低迷の一因です。企業業績がパッとせず、大手証券会社による総会屋への不正利益供与事件が発覚したり、山一、三洋証券が破綻したことなども投資家の投資意欲を減退させています。

　政府はここ数年、株価の下落を防ごうとさまざまな手を打ってきました。経済対策をまとめたり、公的資金を株式市場に投入したり、政府高官が株高誘導の発言をしたりといった具合で、こうした対策は国連のPKO（ピース・キーピング・オペレーション＝平和維持作戦）をもじって株価のPKO（プライス・キーピング・オペレーション＝株価維持作戦）と呼ばれました。

　しかし、みんなが売ろうとしている中で公的資金によって人為的に株価を支えるのには限界があります。結局、PKOも効果はなく、今のところ株価が反騰する兆しは見えません。日本を覆う金融不安が解消され、景気回復の見通しが立ち、企業業績が回復するのを待つしかないようです。

relationships with have also left the market as they try to make up for losses as corporate results deteriorate.

One reason for the low level of stock prices is that the lack of potentially profitable domestic investments has led companies to invest overseas. Continued poor company results, the payment of illegal profits to *sokaiya* (corporate racketeers) by major securities houses, and the failures of Yamaichi Securities Co., Ltd. and Sanyo Securities Co., Ltd. have put off investors from returning to the markets.

The government has for a number of years tried various means to prevent stocks falling. It has set new economic policies, used public funds to intervene in the markets, and its officials have also tried to "talk up" the markets. These have been nicknamed, Price Keeping Operations (PKO) after the United Nations' peace keeping operations.

Using public funds to artificially support share prices in markets where everyone else is selling shares has its limitations. The result has been that the PKO efforts have been ineffectual. Currently, there are still no signs of a rebound. The financial crisis that is hanging over Japan is not disappearing. Japan will have to wait until economic recovery is forecast and corporate results improve before its markets will begin to move upwards and recover.

• 28

Question | 日本の「土地神話」は健在ですか？

Answer | 東京、大阪など6大都市圏の商業地の地価は現在、バブルがピークだった1991年秋の約4分の1、住宅地も半値近い水準まで下がりました。「地価は永遠に下がることはない」という「土地神話」は完全に過去のものになりました。

日本では戦後、地価は一時的に横這いになることはあっても長期的には上昇を続けてきました。特に60年代から70年代はじめにかけては上昇幅が大きく、国民の間に土地神話が定着するようになったのです。

この土地神話を背景に低金利・カネ余り現象も手伝って起きた空前の土地投機ブームがバブルでした。バブル崩壊で多くの企業の経営が行き詰まり、金融機関は不良債権を抱えました。

個人も例外ではなく、バブル期に高値で一戸建て住宅やマンションを購入した人たちは、その後の値下がりで「含み損」を抱えて苦しんでいます。損が出るので売るに売れず、年収の2、3倍にも相当するローンの支払いに耐えきれずに自己破産に追い込まれる人もいます。

• 28

Q: Does Japan's *tochi-shinwa*, land myth, still exist?

A: The price of commercial land in Japan's largest six cities including Tokyo and Osaka is a quarter of the price it was when the economic bubble was at its peak in 1991. The price of residential land has also fallen to about 50 percent of its peak. The land myth, *tochi-shinwa*, that the price of land in Japan would never fall, is now truly a thing of the past.

After the Second World War land prices temporarily leveled off but over the long-term have always continued to rise. The particularly large increases that started in the 1960s and continued into the 1970s led to the nationwide establishment of the land myth.

The economic background of this myth was low interest rates and surplus cash which caused an unprecedented land speculation boom which ultimately led to the economic bubble. The subsequent bursting of the bubble left many companies in financial deadlock and scores of financial institutes holding non-performing loans.

Individuals were not exempt from this. People who built houses or purchased condominiums during the economic bubble were left suffering large hidden losses or negative equity after the fall. People who could not keep up with their mortgage payments on loans worth 2 or 3 times their annual income and could not sell their properties even if they wanted to because of the losses they faced, were driven to bankruptcy.

　ある調査機関の試算では、90年に購入した分譲マンションは97年9月時点で一戸当たり平均約1900万円の含み損を抱えている計算になり、個人住宅が抱える含み損は日本全体では32兆8000億円に達するといいます。これは例えばスウェーデンの国内総生産（GDP）に匹敵します。

　日本人はいま、土地神話を信じたための高い授業料を払わされているかのようです。

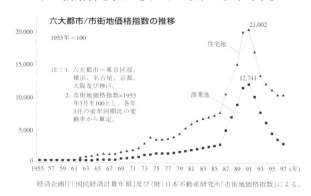

六大都市/市街地価格指数の推移

1955年＝100

注：1. 六大都市＝東京区部、横浜、名古屋、京都、大阪及び神戸。
　　2. 市街地価格指数＝1955年3月を100とし、各年3月の前年同期比の変動率から算定。

住宅地　21,002

商業地　12,741

20,000 / 15,000 / 10,000 / 5,000 / 0

1955 57 59 61 63 65 67 69 71 73 75 77 79 81 83 85 87 89 91 93 95 97（年）

経済企画庁「国民経済計算年報」及び（財）日本不動産研究所「市街地価格指数」による。

• 29

Question　**銀行・証券会社は国際競争力を持っていますか？**

Answer　バブル以前は日本の銀行や証券会社はニューヨークやロンドン、シンガポールなど世界の国際金融市場に次々と進出、豊富なジャパンマネーを国際的な協調融資やプロジェクト融資などに投入、一時は日本の金融機関のオーバープレゼンスが問題になったほどです。

According to one survey new condominiums purchased in 1990 had by September 1997 fallen in value by on average 19 million yen. The hidden losses or negative equity held in residential real estate throughout Japan is now said to amount to a staggering 32 trillion 800 billion yen which is, for example, equivalent to Sweden's annual gross domestic product (GDP).

Japanese people are now paying a high price for believing the land myth.

• 29

Q: Can Japanese banks and stockbrokers compete internationally?

A: Before the economic bubble Japanese financial institutions advanced one after another into the world's international financial centers including New York, London and Singapore. An abundance of Japanese money poured into international projects and syndicate loans. At one point the over-presence of Japanese financial institutions in these markets was considered of international concern.

　しかし、それも今や昔、バブル崩壊後は様変わりで、ニューヨークやロンドンから撤退するところが相次いでいるばかりか、95年ごろからは日本の金融機関がユーロ市場などで資金を調達する場合、「ジャパン・プレミアム」といってヨーロッパやアメリカの一流金融機関に比べて高い金利を支払わされるようになりました。日本の金融機関が抱える大量の不良債権が嫌われたのですが、この状態はまだ続いています。

　実際、日本の銀行の体力は落ちています。利益水準や利益率は世界の主要銀行の後塵を拝しており、国際競争力があるとはとても言えない状態です。

　銀行以上に深刻なのは証券会社です。日本の証券会社はバブルの後始末に加え、総会屋への利益供与というスキャンダルへの対応に追われている間に国際市場で後れをとったばかりか、国内市場でも外国証券会社に抜かれています。

　かつて日本で4大証券と言えば野村、日興、大和、山一でしたが、いま4社と言えばメリルリンチ、モルガン・スタンレー、ゴールドマン・サックス、野村と言われるほどで、日本勢は国内ですら蚊帳の外に置かれています。

Those times now seem like a different era. After the economic bubble burst the situation changed dramatically with a string of institutions retreating from New York and London. From around 1995, Japanese financial institutions borrowing funds in Europe and other financial markets were forced to pay higher rates of interest than equivalent leading American or European institutions in what is known as the "Japan Premium". As international bankers did not want to lend Japanese financial institutions funds due to the enormous amount of bad debts they held and the associated risks. This situation still continues.

It is a fact that the strength of Japanese banks is falling. In terms of profitability and return on capital they are second rate compared to major international banks and it is impossible to say that Japanese banks are currently internationally competitive.

After the banks, it is Japanese stockbrokers who face the most serious difficulties. In addition to having to deal with the aftermath of the collapse of the bubble economy stockbrokers have been trying to cope with scandals associated with illegal profits supplied to *sokaiya*, corporate racketeers. They have been left behind in international markets and have even been overtaken by foreign securities houses in their own domestic market.

People used to refer to the "big four" Japanese stockbrokers, Nomura, Nikko, Daiwa and Yamaichi. But Japanese stockbrokers have fallen so far behind, even in Japan, that when people talk about the "big four" they now mean Merril Lynch, Morgan Stanley, Goldman Sachs and Nomura.

「日本のウォール街・兜町」

ニューヨークのウォール街、ロンドンのシティーに当たるのが東京の証券街「兜町」です。東京証券取引所を中心に大小の証券会社の本店や支店が何百軒と軒を連ね、多くの証券マンが日々の株価に一喜一憂する「相場の町」です。

兜町が証券街として発展したのは、明治11年（1878年）、この地に日本で初めて株式取引所ができたのがきっかけです。

江戸幕府から政権を引き継いだ明治の新政府は、武士を中心とした封建制度の解体に伴う財政難から多くの国債を発行、明治初期にはその国債が両替商らの間で売買されていました。そのうち両替商らの間で「取引所を作ろう」という声が起きて、設立されたのが東京株式取引所です。

株式取引所といっても設立当時は株式会社も少なく、取引の中心は国債でした。その後、日本経済の発展とともに取引所の上場株式も増え、兜町周辺には次々と証券会社ができました。

かつての兜町は、今のように投資家が資産を運用する証券市場というより、むしろ相場師が一攫千金を夢見て勝負する「博打の町」というイメージが強く、戦後も相場師による買い占め事件や仕手戦が頻発しました。

バブル期ピークの88年から89年にかけては株価は高騰に次ぐ高騰で、1日の取引株数も連日のように10億株を超えるなど兜町には熱気が溢れていました。しかしバブル崩壊で株価は低迷、取引株数もピークの3分の1程度に落ち込んでいます。山一証券の破綻などもあり、近ごろは証券マンの表情も沈みがちです。

Kabutocho: The Japanese Wall Street

Tokyo's equivalent of New York's Wall Street, or the City in London, is the financial center Kabutocho. The Tokyo Stock Exchange is located in the center of Kabutocho surrounded by the head offices and branch offices of hundreds of large and small stockbrokers. It is a trading town where stockbrokers' moods are dictated day to day by fluctuations in share prices.

Kabutocho began to develop as a stockbroking area in the 11th year of the Meiji Period in 1878, following the establishment of Japan's first stock exchange.

The new Meiji government who took over from the Edo Shogunate issued a lot of government bonds as part of their efforts to dismantle the feudal system, built around Samurai, which had financial problems. At the start of the Meiji period these bonds were bought and sold by commercial money changers which eventually led to calls by money changers for a trading area to be set up. Subsequently, the Tokyo Stock Exchange was established.

There were very few stocks at the time and despite being called a stock exchange most trading centered around government bonds. As the Japanese economy developed over the years and the number of companies floating their stocks on the Exchange increased, stockbroking firms were set up one after another in Kabutocho.

Formerly, Kabutocho had a strong image as a place where speculators dreamed of making fortunes at a stroke in a "gambling town" rather than a professional exchange where investors managed assets. After the Second World War speculators frequently tried to corner the market and manipulate stocks in speculative battles.

During the height of the economic bubble between 1988 and 1989 stocks soared from one high to another. Daily trading volumes of a billion shares continued day after day and Kabutocho overflowed with feverish excitement. But the bubble burst and stock prices slumped. Daily trading volumes fell to one third of their peak. The failure of leading institutions such as Yamaichi Securities Co., Ltd. has left Japan's once supremely confident stockbrokers browbeaten.

日本のおもしろ会社

Exceptional
Japanese Companies

• 30

| Question | 日本で宿命のライバル企業とは？ |

Answer

日本のビジネス界ではトヨタ自動車と日産自動車、キリンビールとアサヒビール、ソニーと松下電器産業、三菱商事と三井物産、朝日新聞と読売新聞などが宿命のライバルといわれています。

　国内シェアで日産がトヨタに迫った1970年代には、販売競争は熾烈を極めました。対抗心も強く、日産車に乗ってトヨタの工場を訪問するなど論外、トヨタ車のタクシーで日産の工場に行ったら門の前で下ろされたという話もありました。

　最近の日産は、トヨタに対しライバル意識をむき出しにすることも少なくなりました。97年11月には軽自動車を含めた販売台数で日産は初めて本田技研工業に抜かれ、3位に転落、むしろ本田がライバルになってきました。

　トヨタも96年、97年と2年連続でシェア40%を割り込み、往年の迫力はありません。ちなみに97年のトヨタの販売台数は200万台でシェアは39.2%、日産は104万台、20.4%でした。

　ビール業界ではキリンがトップ企業として

• 30

Q: Do fierce corporate rivalries exist in Japan?

A: In the Japanese business world corporate rivalries exist between Toyota Motor Corp. and Nissan Motor Corp., Kirin Brewery Co., Ltd. and Asahi Breweries, Ltd., Sony Corp. and Matsushita Electric Industrial Co., Ltd., Mitsubishi Corp. and Mitsui & Co., Ltd., and Asahi Simbun Publishing Co. and the Yomiuri Shimbun. They are all said to be born rivals.

In the 1970s, Nissan tried to encroach on Toyota's domestic market share and an extremely bitter sales battle developed. Antagonism grew and visiting a Toyota factory in a Nissan car became out of the question. Visitors arriving at a Nissan factory in a taxi made by Toyota, at the time were allegedly made to get out of the taxi before entering Nissan's main gate.

The rivalry between Nissan and Toyota, however, rarely breaks out into the open these days. In November 1997, the number of cars sold by Nissan was surpassed by Honda Motor Co., Ltd. for the first time knocking Nissan into the number three spot in Japan. Honda, not Toyota, is probably Nissan's real rival now.

In 1996 and 1997 for two consecutive years Toyota's domestic market share fell below 40 percent. In 1997 Toyota sold 2 million cars in Japan holding on to a market share of 39.2 percent. Nissan, on the other hand, only sold 1.4 million cars with a total market share of 20.4 percent.

In the world of brewing, Kirin proudly held by far the

圧倒的なシェアを誇っていました。72年から85年までの間、国内シェアは60%を超え、業界のガリバーと呼ばれました。アサヒは87年に辛口の「スーパードライ」を発売して追撃を開始、ぐんぐんと差を縮め、97年には月間シェアで一時キリンを抜きトップに躍り出ました。両社は格好のライバルになってきたようです。

• 31

Question　造船会社がお茶を販売する日本式超多角化戦略の狙いは？

Answer　大手造船会社の日立造船は「杜仲」という木の葉をお茶にした「杜仲茶」を発売しました。ダイエットに効くというので一時はブームになり、年間の売上高は約65億円にも達したほどです。

多角化は造船会社だけではありません。大手家電メーカーの三洋電機は、有料老人ホームの経営に乗り出し、コンピューターメーカーの富士通もテレビ電話などを使った老人の在宅ケア支援事業を始めました。

繊維会社のダイワボウはパソコン販売会社を作って成功、パソコン会社の売上高が親会社の売上高をはるかに上回ってしまいました。

largest domestic market share for beer for years. Between 1972 and 1985 it maintained a domestic market share above 60 percent, and was referred to as "Gulliver," the giant, because of its dominant presence. But in 1987, Asahi launched a new dry beer called "Super Dry" and began pursuing market share. The gap between it and Kirin steadily shrank. In 1997, at one point Asahi overtook Kirin in monthly sales jumping to the top position in terms of market share for the first time. Both companies now seem cast as rivals.

• 31

Q: **What is the aim behind Japanese style super-diversification strategies which allow shipbuilders to sell tea?**

A: The major shipbuilder Hitachi Zosen Corp. uses leaves from the so-called *tochu* tree to make tea which it sells as *tochu* tea. The tea, which is said to encourage weight loss, became extremely fashionable as a diet drink at one point reaching annual sales of 6.5 billion yen.

Diversification in Japan is not limited to shipbuilders. The large electrical appliance manufacturer Sanyo Electric Co., Ltd. has embarked on managing for profit old-age homes and the computer manufacturer Fujitsu Ltd. is using video phones and other appliances to run support services to care for the aged who live at home.

The textile company Daiwabo Co., Ltd. succeeded in setting up a personal computer retailing company which now has annual sales higher than its own. Diversification by

鉄道会社のＪＲ東日本がスーパー経営に乗り出したり、世界最大の鉄鋼メーカー、新日本製鉄が観葉植物の販売をはじめたり、キリンビールが貧血の治療薬など製造事業に進出したりと、日本企業の多角化はとどまるところを知りません。

　企業の繁栄は永久には続きません。どんな事業にも栄枯盛衰はあります。日本でも石炭や紡績業などが衰退していきました。衰退する前に何か新しい事業に乗り換えないと企業の発展はおろか、存続まで危うくなります。そうした危機感が企業経営者をして新規事業、多角化へと駆り立て、なりふり構わぬ日本式超多角化路線となるのです。

　鐘紡はかつては日本を代表する大繊維会社でした。いまや売上高の半分近くは化粧品が占めており、若い人の間では化粧品メーカーとしての方が有名です。これは多角化でうまく変身した例でしょう。

Japanese companies seems to know no bounds with the railway company East Japan Railway Co. trying its hand at supermarket management, Nippon Steel Corp. the world's largest steel maker selling nursery plants and Kirin Brewery Co., Ltd. advancing into pharmaceuticals, selling and manufacturing drugs for the treatment of anemia and other disorders.

Businesses do not always continue to thrive and no matter what the business is it will face ups and downs. In Japan, like many other countries, industries including coal mining and yarn spinning have been in decline for a number of years. Unless companies reinvent themselves by transferring their activities to some new type of enterprise before decline sets in, progress will be retarded and they will merely continue until they reach the point of no return. It is this sense of potential crisis that spurs Japanese managers to set up new businesses and diversify activities leading to this particular Japanese route of diversification.

Kanebo, Ltd. was once one of Japan's leading textile manufacturers. Now almost more than 50 percent of its turnover comes from cosmetics and it is now better known amongst young people in Japan as a cosmetics company. This is one example of a company that has managed to reinvent itself through diversification.

・32

Question　サントリーなどが株式を公開しない理由は何ですか？

Answer　日本のほとんどの大企業は株式を取引所に上場していますが、一部企業は公開していません。

　出光興産、サントリー、竹中工務店、ヤンマーディーゼル、電通、博報堂、JTB（日本交通公社）、日本旅行、西武百貨店、YKKなどが株式を公開していない大企業として有名です。

　電通はいよいよ2001年には東京証券取引所に上場しますが、ほかの会社はいまもなお公開の予定はありません。

　サントリーは、売上高が7000億円を超える日本最大のウイスキーメーカーですが、株式の90％近くを創業家である鳥井家の資産管理会社が保有する同族会社で、代々の社長も鳥井家出身者が務めています。

　鳥井信一郎社長によると、ウイスキーは原料を仕込んでから出荷するのに10年から15年かかり、上場すれば配当を維持するために短期的な利益を追求せざるを得ないこともあり、

• **32**

Q: Why are shares of some major Japanese corporations, like Suntory Ltd., not traded on the stock exchange?

A: In Japan, with the exception of a few leading companies, the stocks of most leading corporations are traded on the stock exchange. Some leading companies are, however, famous for not making their stocks public.

These include: Idemitsu Kosan Co., Ltd., Suntory Ltd., Takenaka Komuten Corp., Ltd., Yanmar Diesel Engine Co., Ltd., Dentsu Inc. Hakuhodo Inc. Japan Travel Bureau, Inc. (JTB), Nippon Travel Agency Co., Ltd. the Seibu Department Stores, Ltd., and YKK Corp.

Shares in Dentsu, one of the world's largest advertising agencies, will finally be made public in 2001 on the Tokyo Stock Exchange. But none of the other companies plans to go public in the near future.

Suntory has an annual turnover of more than 700 billion yen and is Japan's largest whiskey distiller. But close to 90 percent of the company's shares are owned by the family of its founder and are held by the Torii family investment management company. For generations the president of Suntory has come from the Torii family.

According to Shinichiro Torii, the current president of Suntory, it takes between 10 and 15 years from when the brewing process begins until a whiskey can be shipped to customers. The company has not been made public because

それは事業の性格にそぐわない、というのが
公開しない理由だそうです。

出光興産も売上高が2兆円を超える巨大石油
会社ですが、資本金はわずか10億円。やはり
株式は出光家の関係団体がほとんどを所有す
る同族会社で、現社長の出光昭氏は「経営は
人が資本、外部から資本を導入する考えはな
い」と言っています。

他の非公開企業も同族会社が多く、創業家
が大部分の株式を持っており、経営への外部
の介入を嫌がるのが非公開の理由の一つと考
えられます。

• 33

Question　**ガーデニング・ブームの背景は？**

Answer　いま日本ではイギリス式コテッジガーデン風
の庭づくりや庭いじりなど「ガーデニング」
がブームになっています。郊外には大型の園
芸店が続々と店開きし、鉢植えの草花や観葉
植物が好調な売れ行きです。ハーブも再び人
気を呼んでいます。

ブームの理由の一つは「ガーデニング」と
いうネーミングにあります。日本語で「園芸」
や「庭いじり」というと、中年世代以上の趣

if its shares were floated it would have to pursue short-term profits to maintain dividend payments, which would not suit the long-term character of its business.

Idemitsu Kosan Co., Ltd., a major Japanese oil company, also has a very high turnover of more than 2 trillion yen. But it is only capitalized at 1 billion yen with the majority of its shares held by companies or organizations controlled by the Idemitsu family. "In business a company's capital is its staff and we are not considering bringing in new capital from outside," the current president of the company, Akira Idemitsu, says.

Many of the other Japanese companies which are not publicly traded are also family businesses, where the founding family owns a majority stake. Strong resistance from these families is thought to be the one of the main reasons why the companies have not been made public.

• 33

Q: What is the Japanese gardening boom all about?

A: Currently, there is a gardening boom in Japan with English style so-called cottage gardens and other styles of gardening becoming increasingly popular. In the suburbs of major cities gardening shops and nurseries have opened one after another; potted flowering plants and green plants sell extremely well. Growing herbs has also become popular again.

One of the reasons behind this boom is the branding of this as "gardening." The Japanese words for gardening, *engei* and *niwaijiri*, conjure up the image of a hobby held by elderly

味とみられ、若い人は見向きもしません。それが「ガーデニング」というカタカナになると新鮮なイメージになるのか、若い人が急に関心を持ち始め、ブームにつながりました。

こうしたブームに目を付けたのが、食品メーカーなどバイオ技術を持つ企業です。サッポロビールはコチョウランの生産に力を入れ、遺伝子組み替え技術を応用した希少価値がある品種の開発に取り組むなど、アグリバイオ技術を持った企業が次々にこの分野に参入しています。

不況に悩む不動産各社もブームにあやかろうと、大型テラスや専用庭のついたマンションやイギリス風の庭付き住宅などを売り出しています。大手出版社はガーデニング関係の雑誌を創刊、民間カルチャースクールはガーデニング講座を設け、旅行会社はイギリスの有名庭園を訪ねるパック旅行を企画するなど、ガーデニング市場は確実に広がっています。

• 34

Question｜**世界市場で高いシェアを誇る会社は？**

Answer｜オートバイ業界ではホンダ、ヤマハ発動機、スズキの3社が世界市場をほぼ独占、自動車や

and middle-aged people and not an activity attractive to young people. The use of the English word gardening in the *katakana* alphabet creates a fresh image which has quickly attracted the attention of young people and led to the current boom.

The first companies to notice this boom were food product manufacturers and companies with biotechnology related investments. Sapporo Breweries Ltd. started concentrating efforts on producing moth orchids and began applying transgenic technologies to develop rare and valuable kinds of flowers. Other companies with agrobiotechnology related know-how have also moved into the field.

Real estate companies suffering from the current economic down-turn watched this boom develop and are now intent on sharing some of this new found prosperity. They have started building and selling apartments with large terraces and houses with so-called English style private gardens. Major publishing companies have launched gardening related magazines and private "culture schools" have even started gardening related courses. Travel agencies have set up specialist gardening package holidays including trips to England, with visits to famous English gardens. The market for gardening related goods and services is definitely broadening.

• 34

Q: Which Japanese companies boast exceptionally high overseas market shares?

A: In the motorcycle industry three Japanese companies Honda Motor Co., Ltd. Yamaha Motor Co., Ltd. and Suzuki

家電製品でも日本メーカーの名は海外でよく知られていますが、こうした大手企業だけでなく、中堅企業でも世界で圧倒的なシェアを誇る企業が結構あります。

　半導体のウエハーは、直径約5センチ、厚さ約20ミクロン（1ミクロンは1000分の1ミリ）の薄い砥石を使って切断します。その砥石を組み込んだ半導体ウエハー切断装置で世界市場の70％のシェアを占めているのは、東京に本社を置くディスコで、国内では90％のシェアを誇っています。

　写真店が使っている小型の自動現像機（ミニラボ）で、やはり世界市場の50％のシェアを握っているのは、和歌山市のノーリツ鋼機です。社員1200人強の会社ですが、この分野では富士写真フイルムなど大手メーカーを圧倒しています。

　日東電工は、液晶モニター用の偏光フィルムで世界の60％のシェアを維持しています。ファナックは、数値制御（NC）工作機械で世界の50％、国内70％のシェアを占め、マブチモーターも自動車や音響機器などに使われる小型モーターでは世界の50％以上のシェアを誇っています。TDKは、フェライトと磁気テープのトップメーカーです。

　衣類などのファスナー、これは世界48ヵ国に工場を持つYKKがほぼ世界市場を独占しています。

Motor Corp. practically have global monopolies. Japanese automobile and electronics manufacturers are also well-known overseas. But it is not just large Japanese companies that are doing well internationally; many medium sized companies also boast overwhelmingly large international market shares for their products.

For example, semiconductor chips are cut using grind-stone which is approximately 5 centimeters in diameter and 5 microns (1 micron is one thousandth of a millimeter) thick. Cutting-machines inserted with this grindstone made by Disco Corp., headquartered in Tokyo, boast an international market share of 70 percent and a domestic market share of 90 percent.

Noritsui Koki Co., Ltd. based in Wakayama City has grabbed a 50 percent international market share with its Mini Lab automatic photographic developing machines, used by photography shops. Despite only having 1,200 employees it has managed to surpass big international players in this field, like Fuji Photo Film Co., Ltd.

Nitto Denko Corp. is holding onto a 50 percent international market share in polarization film used in liquid crystal displays. Fanuc Ltd. commands a 50 percent international and 70 percent domestic market share in numerically controlled machine tools. Mabuchi Motor Co., Ltd., has an international market share exceeding 50 percent for micro motors used in automobiles and audio equipment. TDK Corp., another Japanese company, is the world's number one maker of ferrite and magnetic film and YKK Corp. with factories in 48 countries has a virtual monopoly in zippers.

• 35

Question 町の名前まで変えてしまった会社とは？

Answer トヨタ自動車が本社を置く愛知県豊田市は人口約34万人、アメリカのデトロイトと姉妹都市関係にある「自動車の町」ですが、1920年代までは養蚕・製糸が主要産業の挙母町という小さな町でした。

　養蚕業が衰退して危機を迎えた挙母町は、近くの刈谷にあった豊田自動織機製作所が自動車の工場用地を探していることを聞き、町ぐるみで工場の誘致活動を展開。その努力が実って1938年（昭和13年）にトヨタ自動車工業（現・トヨタ自動車）の工場が町内に完成、自動車の町として新たなスタートを切りました。

　51年には挙母市になりましたが、60年に商工会議所から市名変更の誓願書が出され、検討の結果、61年に市名は豊田市に変更されました。「挙母」が読みにくいというのも理由の一つですが、市の最大の企業であるトヨタの意向が大きく働いたことは間違いありません。

　創業地の名前を社名にとった会社は結構あ

• **35**

Q: Can Japanese companies change the names of cities?

A: The city of Toyota in Aichi Prefecture, where Toyota Motor Corp. has its headquarters, has a population of about 340,000 and is a sister city of Detroit in the United States. It is a "mo-town" (motor town) by any standards but in the 1920s it was a small textile town called Koromo whose main industries were breeding silkworms and spinning silk.

In the late 1920s this small textile town faced a crisis as the silkworm breeding industry fell into decline. After hearing that Toyoda Automatic Loom Works, in the nearby town of Kariya, was looking for a place to set up an automobile manufacturing factory, the whole town worked together to try to persuade the company to locate the factory in its town. Their efforts paid off. In 1938, the Toyota Motor Company (now Toyota Motor Corp.) completed its factory and the town was reborn as a "mo-town".

In 1951, the town became Koromo City but in 1960 the Chamber of Commerce and Industry issued a document calling for the name of the city to be changed. After consideration, the name of the city was changed to Toyota City. One of the reasons was the difficulty in reading the complicated *kanji* characters used in the name Koromo but there is no doubt the city's largest company Toyota had a significant influence on the decision.

There are many cases of companies using the name of

りますが、逆に社名に合わせて市の名前を変
更した例はあまりありません。これも世界3位
の自動車メーカーの実力なのでしょう。ちな
みにトヨタ本社の住所は豊田市トヨタ町1番地
です。

　トヨタ系列の自動車会社、ダイハツ工業の
本社は大阪府池田市にありますが、やはり本
社の住所は池田市ダイハツ町1−1です。

• 36

Question ロケットからパチンコまで手を出す総
合商社の実力度は？

Answer 「ソーゴーショーシャ」といえば、かつてはラ
ーメンからミサイルまであらゆる商品を取り
扱い、商社マンは貿易立国・日本の先兵とし
て世界中を飛び回るビジネスマンの代表選手
とみられていました。
　いまも営業スタイルはそれほど変わっては
いませんが、各社ともバブル期の不動産投資
の失敗や財テクの損失処理に追われ、アジア
経済の破綻なども響き、以前ほどの元気はあ
りません。志望企業としての学生の人気も低
下気味です。

　しかも最近は大手メーカーなどは自社で輸

the place where they are founded as their company name. But there are few examples of the opposite, a town changing its name to suit a corporation. This highlights the power of the world's number three automobile manufacturer. Incidently, the address of Toyota's head office is Toyota City, Toyota Town, Number 1 district.

The Daihatsu Motor Co., Ltd. which is part of the Toyota *keiretsu*, industrial group, has its headquarters in Ikeda City in Osaka Prefecture but its address is Ikeda City, Daihatsu Town, Number 1 Area 1.

• 36

Q: How powerful are Japan's general trading companies that deal in everything from rockets to *pachinko*?

A: *Sogo-shosha*, general trading companies, have at one time or another dealt in all types of products from noddles to missiles. *Shosha-man*, trading company salesmen are viewed as tough corporate soldiers who travel the world representing the trading nation Japan.

Their business style has not changed much in recent years but they are not as active as they once were, as they are still absorbing losses from real estate investments that went wrong during the economic bubble and *zaiteku*, financial engineering investments. They have also been affected by the Asian economic crisis. In parallel, the number of students aspiring to work for Japanese trading companies has also declined.

Moreover, recently major Japanese manufacturers have

出入業務を手がけるようになり、仲介手数料をあてにしていては先細りになるので、各社とも新規事業分野の開拓に必至です。

　一時、各社はパチンコ向けのプリペイドカード事業に熱中しましたが、偽造・変造カード被害の拡大で熱も冷め、最近、狙いをつけているのは情報通信、放送、金融分野です。

　CATVや衛星放送、衛星通信事業、ビッグバンの波に乗ろうと証券や保険事業に手を出そうとしている会社もあります。高齢社会をにらんで医療・薬局などの事業にも参入しています。

　三菱商事と三井物産が石油メジャーと組み、サハリンで投資額100億ドルという石油・天然ガス開発のプロジェクトを進めるなど資源開発にも熱心ですが、大規模プロジェクトの数は減ってくるなど商社を取り巻く経営環境は年々厳しくなってきているようです。

started to do their own importing and exporting making it more of an uphill struggle for trading companies that live off commissions as middlemen. Inevitably this has led many trading companies to start to develop new business activities.

At one point many Japanese trading companies were very enthusiastic about the prepaid card business for *pachinko* but as losses from forgeries and tampered cards mounted this initial enthusiasm wore off. Recently, they have been targeting telecommunications, broadcasting and finance.

Companies are trying their hand at cable television, satellite broadcasting, and satellite telecommunications as well as trying to ride the wave of the Big Bang financial reforms by moving into finance. Japanese trading companies are also carefully watching Japan's rapidly ageing society and are becoming closely involved in the health care and drug store businesses.

Mitsubishi Corp. and Mitsui & Co., Ltd. are showing increasing enthusiasm for developing natural resources. They have tied up with major international petroleum companies and have invested in a 10 billion dollar oil and natural gas project in Sakhalin. But the number of large-scale projects is decreasing, making the business environment for Japan's trading companies more difficult each year.

• 37

Question **株価が高くて有名な会社はどこですか？**

Answer ソニーは昔から株価が高いことで有名でしたが、平均株価が低迷している現在も崩れず、額面50円に対し1万円を超える高値を維持しています。ビデオカメラなどを中心とした好調な業績に加え、出井伸之社長の積極経営も投資家に評価されているようです。

　本田技研工業や富士写真フイルムといった国際優良株も高い株価を維持しています。ゲーム機の任天堂、リースのオリックス、ノンバンクの日栄、ソフト卸のソフトバンク、警備サービスのセコム、コンビニのセブン－イレブン・ジャパンなども5000円から1万円という人気銘柄です。

　大企業ではありませんが、業績が好調な上に特定分野で高いシェアを持っている企業も投資家の人気を集めています。
　磁気テープのTDKや小型モーターのマブチモーター、検出制御機器メーカーのキーエンス、半導体試験装置メーカーのアドバンテスト、空気圧機器メーカーのSMC、半導体メーカーのロームなどです。

• 37

Q: Which Japanese companies are famous for having high stock prices?

A: Sony Corp. has been famous for having a high share price for a long time. Even now when most Japanese shares have slumped its value has held up keeping a price of over 10,000 yen for its shares which have a nominal face value of 50 yen. In addition to good corporate results generated by its products like video cameras, Sony president Nobuyuki Idei's aggressive management style has won praise from investors.

Honda Motor Co., Ltd. and Fuji Photo Film Co., Ltd., both international blue-chip companies, have also managed to maintain high share prices. The video game maker Nintendo Co., Ltd., the leasing company Orix Corp., the non-bank financial company Nichei Finance Co., Ltd. the Japanese software king Softbank Corp., the security service company Secom Co., Ltd. and the high street retailing chain Seven-Eleven Japan Co., Ltd. are all popular shares worth between 5,000 and 10,000 yen.

Shares in companies which are not major corporations but have large market shares in specific fields are also popular amongst investors. Some of these include the magnetic tape manufacturer TDK Corp. the small motor manufacturer Mabuchi Motor Co., Ltd., the manufacturer of detection equipment Keyence Corp., the semiconductor testing device manufacturer Advantest Corp., the compressed oxygen manufacturer SMC Corp. and the semiconductor manufacturer Rohm Co., Ltd.

店頭市場では、96年1月に設立され、97年に店頭公開されたばかりのヤフーがインターネットブームに乗り、額面5万円に対し株価は一時600万円を超えるなど人気を呼んでいます。

一方、経営不安が囁かれるゼネコンなどの株価は50円前後で低迷するなど業績によって株価は2極分化しています。

• 38

Question **海外で成功した会社の代表例は？**

Answer 日本は貿易国ですから、電機や機械、自動車などのメーカーはいずれも輸出に熱心で、円高以降は海外での工場建設にも積極的です。そのため海外で高い評価を受けるなど成功した企業は数多いのですが、その中で代表例を上げるとしたらソニー、松下電器産業、三洋電機、日立製作所などの電機メーカー、それにトヨタ自動車、日産自動車、本田技研工業などの自動車メーカーでしょう。

ニコンやキヤノンなどの日本のカメラも海外では定評があります。毛色の変わったところではファミコン、とくにゲームボーイで有名な任天堂。もともとは京都でトランプや花

On the over-the-counter market Yahoo Japan Corp. which was set up in January 1996 and registered on the market in 1997 is extremely popular. The company is riding the internet boom. Its shares issued with a nominal face value of 50,000 yen peaked at one point at over 6 million yen.

But on the other hand general construction companies, often refered to as *zenekon*, face uncertain futures. Their shares have fallen to below 50 yen creating an extreme polarization in the Japanese stock markets based on performance.

• 38

Q: Which Japanese companies have been successful internationally?

A: Japan is a trading nation whose electronics, machine and automobile manufacturers eagerly export their goods across the globe. After the rise in the value of the yen in the 1980s these manufacturers aggressively set up factories overseas. Many companies have developed strong reputations and have been successful internationally. But the most successful companies probably include the electronics manufacturers: Sony Corp., Matsushita Electric Industrial Co., Ltd. Sanyo Electric Co., Ltd. Hitachi, Ltd., and the automobile manufacturers, Toyota Motor Corp., Nissan Motor Co., Ltd., and Honda Motor Co., Ltd.

Cameras made by Nikon Corp. and Canon Inc. are well established international brands with good international reputations. But Nintendo Co., Ltd., which became famous with its computer games especially its Gameboy toy is a com-

札を作る会社でしたが、今やゲーム機メーカーとして世界的に有名になりました。

　カップヌードルの日清食品も世界の各地に工場を建設、日本の特産品であるインスタントラーメンのカップ麺を世界に普及させました。食品関係では醤油を海外に紹介したキッコーマンも成功した企業といえるでしょう。

　円高の直撃を受けて赤字に転落したのをきっかけに国内の工場を大幅にリストラし、アジアに生産拠点を移して成功した会社もあります。ソニーの子会社で音響機器専門メーカーのアイワです。ミニコンポなど製品の海外生産比率は90％に達し、低価格を武器にミニコンポのトップメーカーにのし上がりました。

• 39

Question	**無借金会社の代表例はどこですか？**
Answer	受取利息・配当金から、支払い利息・割引料を差し引いた金融収支が黒字の事実上の「無借金会社」として最も有名なのはトヨタ自動車です。

pletely different kettle of fish. The company from Kyoto originally made playing cards and *hanafuda* (Japanese traditional playing cards) but is now famous across the world for its computer game machines.

The cup noodle producer Nisshin Food Products Co., Ltd. has built factories all around the world and has spread the unique Japanese product of instant cup noodles throughout the globe. Another company which has been successful in food products is Kikkoman Corp. which introduced soya sauce internationally.

Some companies knocked into the red by the sudden rise in the yen completely restructured their local factories and succeeded by moving their manufacturing bases to other Asian countries. The Sony subsidiary Aiwa Co., Ltd. a specialist audio-equipment manufacturer, is one of these companies: 90 percent of its products including its popular mini-high-fi systems are now manufactured outside Japan. Using low prices as a weapon to compete in international markets Aiwa has developed itself into the world's number one manufacturer of mini-high-fi systems.

• 39

Q: Which are Japan's leading debt free companies?

A: Companies whose financial accounts are in the black when interest received on loans, and dividend payment receipts are subtracted from interest paid on loans, are called *mushakkin-gaisha*, debt free companies. The most famous of these is Toyota Motor Corp.

　97年9月末の現金・預金・有価証券を合計した手元流動性は約1兆5000億円。巨額の金融資産から別名「トヨタ銀行」と呼ばれるほどで、96年度の金融収支はこの低金利下でも年間約640億円の黒字となりました。

　トヨタも1949年の戦後の「ドッジ不況」の際、あわや倒産という事態に追い込まれたことがあります。当時の日銀支店長が民間銀行を説き伏せてシンジケート団を結成、緊急融資をしてくれたので何とか助かりましたが、このときの苦い教訓からトヨタは無借金経営を目指すようになったのです。

　松下電器産業も事実上の無借金経営で知られています。96年度の金融収支はやはり400億円の黒字でした。ゲーム機メーカーの任天堂は名実ともに無借金で、借入金はゼロです。

　逆に日本一の借金王は東京電力。97年9月末の有利子負債は約10兆6700億円に達し、96年度の金融収支は4640億円の赤字でした。発電所など多額の設備投資が必要な電力会社は、東電に限らず軒並み多額の借金を抱えています。

At the end of September 1997, the total amount of liquid assets including cash, savings and securities held by Toyota was 1 trillion 500 billion yen. These vast financial assets led to the company being dubbed the "Toyota Bank." In 1996, despite low Japanese interest rates Toyota earned 64 billion yen from its financial assets alone.

During the Dodge Recession in 1949, the recession caused by the budgetary cuts instigated by Joseph Morrel Dodge, the former American Minister in Japan, Toyota faced potential bankruptcy. The head of the Nagoya branch office of the Bank of Japan at the time persuaded a number of private companies to set up a syndicate loan. This emergency funding rescued Toyota and it was this early and important lesson which led Toyota into becoming a debt free company.

Matsushita Electric Industrial Co., Ltd. is also known for its debt free management style. In 1996, its profits from its financial holdings were a staggering 40 billion yen. The game maker Nintendo Co., Ltd. is also famous for borrowing no money at all.

On the other hand Japan's most indebted company is the Tokyo Electric Power Co., Inc. In September 1997, its interest bearing liabilities reached 10 trillion 670 billion yen. In 1996 the company's accounts were approximately 464 billion yen in the red. The Tokyo Electric Power Co., Inc., which needs to make expensive capital investments in power generators, is by no means the only Japanese power company with large debts.

「意外に知らない社名の由来」

日本ではトヨタ自動車や松下電器産業など創業者の名前から取った社名が多いのですが、楽器メーカーのヤマハも創業者、山葉寅楠の名前からとりました。最初の商号は「山葉風琴製作所」、その後社名は「日本楽器製造」となりましたが、ブランド名としては「ヤマハ」を残し、その後社名もヤマハに変更しました。

日本を代表する演劇・映画会社で、古くは小津安二郎監督、現役では山田洋次監督らの一連の作品で知られる松竹は、京都生まれの双子、白井松次郎と大谷竹次郎兄弟が創立したので松竹と名付けられました。

ソニーの元の社名は東京通信工業。外国人が発音しにくいため1955年に商品に「SONY」の商標をつけました。音を意味するラテン語の「SONUS」(ソヌス)と、英語で小さい子供を意味する「SONNY」を掛け合わせた造語で、その後社名になりました。

シャープは、創業者の早川徳次氏が発明した繰り出し鉛筆「エバー・レディ・シャープ・ペンシル」からとりました。無名の町工場はその後、家電業界に進出、社名は早川兄弟商会金属文具製作所から早川金属工業、早川電機工業と変わり70年からシャープに。

キヤノンは、創業者グループの一人が観音教の信者で、試作したカメラを「カンノン」(KWANON)と命名、発売の段階で、聖典などの意味を持つ「キヤノン」(CANON)としたのが由来です。発音通り「キャノン」としないのは、大文字の「ヤ」の方がデザイン的に調和が取れているためとか。

The scarcely known origin of Japanese corporate names

The names of many companies in Japan like Toyota Motor Corp. and Matsushita Electric Industrial Co,. Ltd. come from their founders. The musical instrument maker Yamaha Corp. gets its name from its founder Torakusu Yamaha. Originally, it was called the Yamaha Organ Manufacturing Plant but it later changed to Nippon Gakki Co., Ltd. using the name Yamaha only to brand its products. Eventually, the company changed its name to Yamaha.

The name of the leading Japanese theater and film production company Shochiku Co., Ltd., famous for its films directed by the celebrated directors Yasujiro Ozu and Yoji Yamada, comes from the names of Matsujiro Shirai and Takejiro Otani the twin brothers from Kyoto, who founded the company.

Sony Corp.'s original name was Tokyo Telecommunications Engineering Corporation. As non-Japanese people had trouble pronouncing the name, in 1955 they started placing the trademark Sony on products. The name is derived from a combination of the Latin word *sonus* for sound and the English word sonny meaning young boy. Afterwards it became the company's name.

Sharp Corp. takes its name from automatic mechanical pencils called "ever ready sharp pencils", which were invented by its founder Tokuji Hayakawa. The unknown village factory run by Hayakawa moved into home electrical appliances changing its name from the Hayakawa Brothers Commercial Metallic Stationery Manufacturing Plant to Hayakawa Metallic Manufacturing to Hayakawa Electronics Manufacturing and eventually in the 1970s to Sharp.

One of the founders of the Canon Group was a believer in Kannon the goddess of mercy. He christened an experimental camera he was working on Kwanon. When the product reached its final stage of development and was ready to be sold its name was changed to canon which can amongst other things mean holy book. The spelling of the name was changed for design purposes.

日本の会社の不思議

Strange Facts about
Corporate Japan

・40

Question　**学校まで作る会社の実力とは？**

Answer　国内や海外の有名大学などに多額の寄付をする日本企業は結構ありますが、中には寄付だけでは満足せず、国内に大学そのものをつくった会社もあります。

　愛知県にある豊田工業大学は、トヨタ自動車が社会貢献活動の一貫として1981年に創設した大学です。日本の将来を担う技術者を育てるというのが、建学の理念で、体験的授業と少人数教育が特徴です。トヨタがスポンサーですので、授業料は国立大学並みに安く、手厚い奨学金制度もあります。

　ダイエーも中内功会長兼社長が提案して88年、ダイエーの地元神戸市に流通科学大学を設立しました。「流通産業を科学する全く新しい理念の大学」（中内氏）というのが売り物で、流通を中心にサービス産業全般やファイナンス分野などを教育、研究のテーマにしています。

　もっとユニークなのは、松下電器産業の故松下幸之助氏が80年に神奈川県に創設した「松下政経塾」でしょう。これは大学でも研究

• **40**

Q: Do Japanese companies set up and run their own schools?

A: Many Japanese companies donate large sums of money to famous universities in Japan and overseas but some companies, not satisfied only with making donations, have gone as far as setting up their own universities in Japan.

The Toyota Technological Institute in Aichi Prefecture was established in 1981 as part of Toyota Motor Corp.'s contributions-to-society program. The ideology behind the university is to educate technicians for the future of Japan. Some of the special characteristics of the institute are its practical experience based courses and the small size of its classes. As the institute is sponsored by Toyota the tuition fees are as low as those at national universities and generous grants are also available.

Daiei, Inc. has also set up a university following a proposal by Isao Nakauchi, the company's president and chairman. In 1988, in Kobe where Daiei is based, it established the University of Marketing and Distribution Sciences. The concept of a university treating distributive trades as a science was completely new in Japan and is the school's key selling point. The university concentrates its research and educational themes on service industries including distribution and finance.

Probably the only school of its type is the Matsushita Institute of Government and Management, set up in 1980 in Kanagawa Prefecture, by Konosuke Matsushita. It is neither

所でもありません。名前の通り私設の政治家、経営者養成所です。

　政治家や企業経営者を目指す若者を全国から公募、2年から3年、実践教育を通じて夢の実現を支援します。在塾中は月額31万円の研修手当と一人当たり100万円から300万円の実践研究活動費が支給されます。こうした手厚い支援を受けて卒業生約160人（98年現在）からは国会議員や県会議員、市長などが多数輩出しています。

・41

Question | **日本のビジネスは神頼み？**

Answer | ものを作って売る、仕入れて売る、どちらにしても商売は自分の努力だけでは超えられない「運」や「不運」に左右されることがあります。そこで日本の商人は昔から縁起をかつぎ、神様にも商売繁盛をお願いすることが多かったようです。

　この伝統は現在も引き継がれており、日本の全国各地には商売の神様を祭る神社がたくさんあります。関西では京都の伏見稲荷や大阪の今宮戎神社が有名です。

a university nor a research institute. As its name suggests it is a private center for cultivating politicians and managers.

It recruits young people from all over Japan who have ambitions of becoming politicians or captains of industry and over a 2 or 3 year period tries to help them realize their dreams through practical training and support. While at the institute individuals receive a research allowance of 310,000 yen per month and a practical research activity allowance of between 1 million and 3 million yen. As of 1998, about 160 people have been the recipients of this generous support and have graduated from the institute. Many of them are now members of the national parliament or local legislators or mayors of Japanese cities.

• 41

Q: Do Japanese companies pray to the gods?

A: No matter what type of business you are involved in, whether it is making and selling products or selling supplies, there are certain aspects that are out of your control, which are governed by luck or misfortune. Since ancient times Japanese merchants have been superstitious and have often prayed to special deities of business prosperity.

This tradition has been passed down to today's generation of businessmen and no matter where you go in Japan there are many shrines dedicated to the gods and deities of business prosperity. In the Kansai region in Kyoto City the Fushimi Inari shrine and in Osaka City the Imamiya Ebisu shrine are famous.

　今宮戎神社では、毎年1月10日の「十日戎」には、商運を呼び込む「福笹」を買い求める中小企業の経営者、商店主、サラリーマンらが多数参拝に訪れます。

　日本のウォール街といわれる兜町には兜神社があり、毎年春の祭日には証券界のトップが株式相場の上昇を祈願します。

　中小企業の事務所や商店の店先などには、商売の神様を祭る神棚を設けているところが多く、経営者は毎朝、神棚に向かい商売繁盛を祈願します。大企業でも社長室に神棚を設けたり、構内に小さな社を建てて創業者らを祭っているところもあります。

　企業が本社ビルや工場を建設するときなどは、必ず工事の無事と企業の繁栄を祈るため神主を招き、土地の神様を祭る地鎮祭を執り行います。いくら近代的な組織になってもそこで働く日本人社員のメンタリティーはあまり変わっていないようです。

Every year on 10 January at the Imamiya Ebisu shrine during the *Toka-ebisu* period, owners of small and medium sized companies, shopkeepers, and *salarymen* visit the shrine to purchase blessings for business success.

Even in Kabutocho, Japan's Wall Street, there is a small shrine. Every spring during the shrine's annual festival top executives from Japan's leading finance companies visit the shrine and pray for the stock market to rise.

In the administrative offices of small and medium sized companies and outside shops in Japan you can often see *kamidana*, small household *Shinto* shrines. Many owners worship in front of these each morning before starting work. *Kamidana* are sometimes also found in the presidents' offices of major Japanese corporations and some companies in Japan even build small shrines dedicated to their founders in their offices.

When new headquarter buildings and factories are erected in Japan *Shinto* priests are normally invited to perform a special *Shinto* ceremony before construction begins to purify the building site, to appease the gods of the land, to ensure that the construction takes place without incident and to ensure the prosperity of the company. No matter how modern Japanese organizations become the mentality of the employees working within the companies hardly seems to change.

● 42

Question　日本企業の株式配当率はなぜ低いのですか？

Answer　全上場企業の株価に対する配当金の比率、つまり平均利回りは1%以下です。はっきりした統計はありませんが、欧米企業に比べ日本企業の配当率は低いといわれています。

　理由は、日本企業が伝統的に「安定配当」の考え方を取っているためです。1株当たりの配当金を年間5円と決めたら、企業はその水準をできるだけ維持しようとします。利益が大幅に減ったり、場合によっては実質的に赤字になっても、内部留保を取り崩したりして配当を払おうとする企業が多数あります。逆に利益が増えても配当は増やさず、据え置く傾向があります。

　これに対し欧米では、1株当たり利益の何%を配当に回すかという「配当性向」を基準に、株主に還元する考え方が一般的です。利益が出れば増やすが、減れば配当も減らす、赤字になれば当然ゼロというように柔軟に対応する考え方です。

　欧米流の方が自然ですが、日本では、経営者が経営の責任を取りたくないこともあり、

• 42

Q: Why do Japanese companies pay such low dividends ?

A: The average dividend rate relative to the share price of floated companies in Japan is less than 1 percent. Exact figures do not exist but compared to American and European companies', dividend payments in Japan are extremely low.

This is because Japanese companies have traditionally taken a position of making steady annual fixed dividend payments. Companies who have decided to pay a dividend of 5 yen per share per year try to maintain that rate no matter what. Even if profits decrease significantly or the company goes into the red many companies will dip into financial reserves in order to maintain dividend payments. On the other hand, if profits rise dividend payments are not increased and payments tend to be left unchanged.

In Europe and the United States a certain percentage of profits per share is returned to shareholders in the form of dividends each year. This system of *haitoseiko*, ratio of earnings to dividend payments, makes it standard for corporate profits to be returned to shareholders and is considered standard international practice. If profits increase dividends increase, if profits fall dividend payments fall, and if the company makes a loss dividends will naturally not be paid out under this flexible system.

The European and American systems are more intuitive but perhaps because Japanese managers do not wish to take

安定配当の考え方からなかなか抜け出せません。

しかし、海外の投資家から低配当率に対する批判が高まっており、日本でも92年から「公募増資などをした企業は原則として配当性向30%以上を維持する」という新ルールを導入しました。ルールが適用されるのは、公募増資をしたり、転換社債などを発行した企業だけですが、日本企業も徐々に配当性向主義に向けて動き出しています。

• 43

Question 日本の社長の給料は欧米の社長に比べてなぜ安いのですか？

Answer オーナー経営者を別にすると、日本の大企業の社長の給料は年収ベースで3000万円から7000万円ほどです。年俸5億円、10億円も珍しくないアメリカ企業のトップに比べると慎ましい限りです。

大卒新入社員の月給は20万円程度で、ボーナスを含めて新入社員の年収は300万円から350万円ですから、社長の年収は新入社員の10倍から20倍ということになります。しかも所得税は累進課税ですから税金を差し引いた手

direct responsibility for corporate results they are reluctant to breakaway from the system of paying steady fixed dividends.

However, criticism from international investors over low dividends rates is increasing. In 1992, a new rule was introduced in Japan which stipulates that companies increasing public funding of their enterprises have to, as a matter of principle, maintain more than a 30 percent ratio of earnings to dividends. This rule only applies to companies increasing public capital and those issuing convertible corporate bonds. But nevertheless, Japanese companies are beginning to move in the direction of paying annual dividends based on earnings.

• 43

Q: Are the presidents of Japanese companies paid less than their counterparts in the United States and Europe?

A: With the exception of owner-managers most presidents of major Japanese companies earn between 30 million and 70 million yen per year. This is modest compared to the United States where it is not unusual for top executives in major international companies to earn 500 million or even 1 billion yen per year.

In Japan new graduate recruits generally earn about 200,000 yen per month and if you include their annual bonuses their annual salary is in the order of between 3 and 3.5 million yen. A company president's annual income is about 10 or 20 times this. However, income tax in Japan is a progressive

取り収入の差はもっと縮まります。給料の面では日本は極めて格差が小さい平等社会といえます。

そもそも平等主義が日本型経営の特徴です。少数の優秀な人材をエリートとして育てて、エリートが出世の階段を駆け上ってトップに就くという仕組みにはなっていません。

たいていの会社では新入社員は全員ほぼ平等のチャンスを与えられます。その後、課長や部長に昇進するたびに少しずつふるいにかけられ、最後に残ったものが役員や社長になるのです。昇進に伴って同じ年齢、同じ学歴でも次第に給料の差は広がりますが、差といっても微々たるものです。

第二次大戦前は新入社員、幹部、社長のそれぞれの給料の差はもっと大きかったようです。戦後、差が縮まったのは民主主義教育の成果かも知れません。

• **44**

Question スポーツ選手を抱え、美術館を運営する企業の収支勘定は？

Answer 有名スポーツ選手を社員に抱えるのは、企業イメージや社員のプライドを高める効果があるからです。

98年の長野冬季五輪で、スキージャンプの

tax and the gap in actual take-home pay after tax is much less. From the point of view of salaries Japan is an egalitarian society with an extremely small disparity in earnings.

Egalitarianism is one of the characteristics of Japanese management. It is not the type of system where a minority of talented individuals are raised as an elite group and are on a guaranteed fast track route to the top.

At the majority of Japanese companies new recruits are given equal opportunities. Subsequently, after they have been promoted to section heads or departmental heads a gradual screening process begins and the individuals who remain end up becoming directors or the president of the company. As people are promoted the degree of difference in salary between individuals of the same age and academic backgrounds widens but this difference is minimal.

Before the Second World War the difference in salaries of new recruits, executives and presidents was much larger. But after the war this shrank probably as the result of the new education system based on democratic principles.

• 44

Q: How do Japanese companies justify the expense of hiring famous athletes and running art museums?

A: Companies in Japan employ famous athletes to motivate their staff and improve their corporate image.

According to various surveys, the success at the 1998

　原田雅彦選手や船木和喜選手が大活躍したお
かげで原田選手を抱える雪印乳業や、船木選
手のデサントの企業イメージが非常に良くな
ったという調査結果があります。原田選手の
活躍は、広告費に換算すると数億円という試
算もあるほどです。

　企業イメージが良くなり、優秀な人材が集
まるようになれば、業績向上にも結びつきま
す。

　本田技研工業は93年以来休止していたF−1
レースに復帰することを決めましたが、先端
技術の蓄積に加え、企業文化の育成が狙いと
言っています。 美術館や音楽ホールの運営、
芸術活動支援などの文化活動も企業のイメー
ジアップが狙いです。

　しかし、最近の不況で野球やラグビー、バ
スケットボールなど各種のスポーツチームを
維持するのが難しくなり、廃止に追い込まれ
る名門実業団チームも目立ってきました。

　文化活動でも、セゾングループがリストラ
の一環としてセゾン美術館を99年2月に閉館す
ることになったり、山種証券系の財団が運営
する山種美術館が規模を縮小するなど、だん
だん収支勘定は合わなくなっているようです。

Nagano Winter Olympics of the ski jumpers Masahiko Harada and Kazuyoshi Funaki in winning gold medals for Japan tremendously improved the image of Snow Brand Milk Products Co., Ltd. and Descente, Ltd. which employed the respective ski jumpers. If you convert Harada's success into advertising it was easily worth several hundred million yen.

If a company's image improves it becomes easier to recruit better qualified staff which subsequently improves corporate performance.

In 1993, Honda Motor Co., Ltd. decided to return to Formula One motorcar racing. The company says its aim in returning to the sport is not only to acquire leading-edge technologies but also to build its corporate culture. Companies that run art museums, concert halls or sponsor cultural events and other activities also aim to improve their corporate images.

However, economic recession has made it more difficult for companies to maintain their various sports teams including baseball, rugby and basketball teams. Many famous teams have been disbanded.

The arts have also been negatively affected. The Saison Group will close its museum the Saison Art Museum in February 1999. The Yamatane Securities Co., Ltd. foundation which runs the Yamatane Art Museum has reduced the scale of the museum, highlighting the difficulties Japanese companies are currently having justifying these types of expenses.

• 45

Question | 日本の会社にはなぜ重役が何十人もいるのですか？

Answer | 97年末時点で東証上場企業の取締役数ナンバー1は東京三菱銀行の62人。同行の場合、三菱銀行と東京銀行が合併したこともあり別格ですが、総じて日本の会社の取締役は多く、30人から40人もいる会社はざらです。

　　取締役会は業務執行に関する意思決定の最高機関であり、経営戦略をめぐる活発な討議をする場ですが、これだけ多いと討議に時間がかかり、スピード経営には間に合いません。そこで各社とも常務会や副社長会などで重要事項を事実上決め、取締役会はそれを承認するだけというのが実態です。

　　しかし、国際的な大競争を勝ち抜くにはグローバル・スタンダードに基づいた経営体制の確立が不可欠という判断から、最近は取締役数を大幅に減らす企業が相次いでいます。先陣を切ったのはソニー。97年にそれまで38人いた取締役を一挙に10人に減らしました。東芝も98年に取締役を約3分の1の12人に削減、富士写真フイルム、アイワなども大幅に減らしました。

• **45**

Q: Why do Japanese companies have dozens of directors?

A: At the end of 1997, the company with the largest number of directors on the Tokyo Stock Exchange was the Bank of Tokyo-Mitsubishi Ltd. with 62. This followed the merger of the Bank of Tokyo and the Mitsubushi Bank Ltd. which probably gives the company special status. Nevertheless, Japanese companies have a relatively large number of directors. Companies with between 30 and 40 directors are common.

Board of directors' meetings are the highest corporate decision making bodies and should be a forum for lively debate about corporate strategy and policy. But with such large numbers of directors debate takes time, making it impossible to manage at speed. Many Japanese companies make important decisions at managing director level meetings and vice president meetings which are afterwards, in reality, just approved or rubber stamped by the board of directors.

However, to survive international mega-competition the introduction of management systems in Japan based on global standards is now thought to be essential. Recently, the number of directors at Japanese companies is being reduced by more and more organizations. Sony Corp. led the way. In 1997, it reduced the number of its directors from 38 to 10 in one swoop. In 1998 Toshiba Corp. reduced the number of its directors by a third to 12 and Fuji Photo Film Co., Ltd. and Aiwa Co., Ltd. also reduced the number of their directors significantly.

ただ日本では取締役はサラリーマンの出世競争の最終ゴールです。欧米企業ほどではありませんが、取締役になれば収入もぐんと増えます。数が減れば取締役への道はますます狭き門になるわけですから、「いつかは取締役に」と願うサラリーマンにとって「重役のリストラ」の評判はあまり良くありません。

・**46**

Question　**建設会社の談合はなぜ起きるのですか？**

Answer　信じられないでしょうが、日本には約56万の建設会社があります。ほとんどは中小企業で、そこで働く従業員は700万人近くに達し、就業者全体の1割以上を占めています。

　人口1000人の村に建設会社が10社あり、村民の数人に一人は建設業に従事しているところもあります。小さな村に10社も建設会社が存在できるのは、国や地方自治体の公共投資のおかげです。国や自治体は、橋や道路建設など年間数十兆円の公共投資を実施しており、建設会社は村内や近くで行われる事業を受注して儲けているのです。

However, becoming a company director is the pinnacle of success and the ultimate goal of Japanese salaried workers. Making it to director level also means a large increase in salary. Salary levels are not as high as directors at American or European companies but nevertheless the increase is significant. If the number of director positions is reduced the route to a seat on the board of directors becomes even narrower. This current restructuring of the board of directors of Japanese companies is not popular amongst salaried workers who dream of becoming directors themselves one day.

• 46

Q: Why does price fixing exist amongst Japanese construction companies?

A: It is hard to believe but there are about 560,000 construction companies in Japan. The majority of them are small or medium sized enterprises. Almost 7 million people work for these companies, occupying about 10 percent of Japan's total working population.

There are cases of small Japanese villages with populations of 1,000 people which contain 10 construction companies. Amongst the villagers one in every few people will be employed in the construction industry. The reason why 10 construction companies can exist in such small villages is due to public investment programs carried out by national and local governments. The national and local governments have spent trillions of yen of public funds over the years building roads and bridges. Construction companies have profited from

　小さな村ですと公共投資を何年も続けると社会資本の整備は終わるはずですが、そうなると会社は倒産、村民が失職しますので、必要な社会資本整備が終わっても使い道のなさそうな道路や橋、建物などを次々に建設しています。

　こうした政府・自治体と建設会社のもたれ合いの風土が談合を生んでいます。役所は予算を消化すればよく、費用には鷹揚です。だから入札で建設業者は談合し、高値で工事を受注、利益を分けあうのです。　大手業者が、受注した仕事を丸ごと下請けに回しマージンを取る「丸投げ」なども横行しています。

　国民の間でこうした税金の無駄遣いに対する批判が高まっていますが、建設省や地方自治体などは、退職後の職員を建設会社に引き受けてもらっている弱みもあるので、改善には消極的です。

participating in projects taking place near their villages.

Public investment schemes, continuing over a number of years, should come to an end when the necessary local infrastructure is developed but if this were to happen the construction companies in small villages would go bankrupt and villagers would become unemployed once investments stopped. So even after construction of the necessary infrastructure is complete, for political reasons construction of bridges and roads, which do not have any apparent necessary use, continue.

This relationship between the state, local governments and construction companies leads to price fixing. Government offices are not concerned about the overall cost of each project as their objective is to spend their budgets. Therefore construction companies consult each other before bidding for contracts and win highly priced new construction projects. They subsequently share the profits amongst themselves. Major companies pass on complete projects to subcontractors while keeping a margin for themselves in what is know as *marunage*.

Criticism from the general public about the waste of taxpayers money is increasing. But officials from the construction ministry and local governments often join the payrolls of construction companies on retirement, making change very difficult if not impossible.

「曲がり角の春闘」

日本の労働組合は毎年春、一斉に賃上げ闘争を行います。1956年から始まった伝統行事で、例年1月から2月にかけて自動車、電機、鉄鋼、造船など主要産業の各労働組合が相次いで経営陣に賃上げ要求書を提出、何回かの交渉を経て3月中旬ごろに経営陣が一斉に賃上げ回答を労組に示します。

98年春闘の賃上げ実績は民間主要企業で平均8323円、賃上げ率は2.66%でした。

日本の企業は4月から新たな経営年度に入る会社がほとんどです。このため新年度を前にした春に賃上げ闘争が行われるようになり、春の季語として「春闘」という言葉が定着しました。

70年代ごろまでは過激な労組も多く、鉄道関係労組などが賃上げを不満として、しばしば交通ストを打ちましたが、最近は大規模なストはほとんどなくなりました。

かつて賃上げ一本槍だった春闘も、最近は賃上げと併せて勤務時間の短縮、つまり「時短」要求が大きな柱になっています。例年の春闘の主役である鉄鋼業界は98年から2年分の賃上げを1回の交渉で決める「複数年協定方式」に移行するなど改革の動きもあり、春闘は曲がり角を迎えています。

民間主要企業の賃上げ実績

	賃上げ額（円）	賃上げ率（%）
1970年	9,166	18.5
75年	15,279	13.1
80年	11,679	6.74
85年	10,871	5.03
90年	15,026	5.94
91年	14,911	5.65
92年	13,662	4.95
93年	11,077	3.89
94年	9,118	3.13
95年	8,376	2.83
96年	8,712	2.86
97年	8,927	2.90
98年	8,323	2.66

The Spring Labor Offensive: A turning point

Every spring Japanese labor unions simultaneously start a wage increase offensive. This began in 1956. Under this now traditional event, each year between January and February the labor unions from the main industries including motor manufacturing, electronics, steel and shipbuilding, send their demands for wage increases to management one by one. After several rounds of negotiations in mid March management at companies in these sectors simultaneously announce their response to the unions.

In 1998 the average wage increase at major private sector companies was 8,323 yen, an increase of 2.66 percent.

The majority of Japanese companies start their new financial year in April. Due to this, in spring just before the new financial year begins, demands for higher wages are made. The word *shunto*, spring labor offensive, is now fixed as a word associated with the season spring.

In the 1970s, there were many radical unions for example, the railways workers union, which started transport strikes when they were dissatisfied with their pay increases. Recently, however, large scale strikes are no longer common in Japan.

Previously, the *shunto* was all about increases in wages. But more recently demands for increases in wages are combined with requests for *jitan*, reductions in working hours, which has become a key issue in these negotiations. Each year the steel industry plays a critical role in the *shunto*. In 1998, they decided on wage increases for a two year period in one set of negotiations thus moving to a multi-year agreement system, which leave the *shunto* at an uncertain turning point.

日本で成功するには

Succeeding in Japan

• 47

Question	日本で成功した代表的な外国企業はどこですか？
Answer	日本に進出している外資系企業は5000社前後といわれます。成功の尺度として所得ランキングをみますと、日本コカ・コーラ、日本アムウェイ、日本IBM、富士ゼロックス、ゼネラル石油、インテルジャパン、ネスレ日本、萬有製薬、昭和シェル石油などが上位を占めています。

　ほとんどが外国企業の子会社ですが、萬有製薬のようにもともと日本の会社だったのが、アメリカの医薬品メーカー、メルク社の傘下に入り、成功した例もあります。

　日本マクドナルドも非常に成功したケースでしょう。1971年にマクドナルドと藤田田氏が合弁で設立した会社で、設立以来、藤田氏が社長を務め、国内店舗3000店の大企業に成長しました。上場すれば株の時価総額は1兆円を超えるといわれる優良会社で、マクドナルドの海外展開の中で最も成功したケースとして知られています。

　イトーヨーカ堂が株式の50％以上を持っているので外資系ではありませんが、セブン–イレブン・ジャパンも成功し、セブン–イレブンの本家、アメリカのサウスランド社を買収し

• 47

Q: Which foreign companies are succeeding in Japan?

A: There are said to be just under 5,000 foreign companies building their business presences in Japan. If one measures success by ranking companies by revenue Coca-Cola (Japan) Co., Ltd., Amway Japan Ltd., IBM Japan Ltd., Fuji Xerox Co., Ltd., General Sekiyu K.K., Intel Japan Co., Ltd., Nestlé Japan Co., Ltd., Banyu Pharmaceutical Co., Ltd. and Showa Shell Sekiyu K.K. occupy the top slots.

The majority of these are subsidiaries of overseas multinational companies. But there are examples like Banyu, originally a Japanese company, which later became a successful affiliate of Merck & Co., Ltd., an American pharmaceutical company.

McDonald's (Japan) Co., Ltd. is an extremely successful case. In 1971, McDonald's and Den Fujita set up a joint venture. Since then Fujita has been president of the company and it has grown into a major corporation with over 3,000 restaurants in Japan. It is a blue-chip company which is said to be worth more than 1 trillion yen if it were made public. It is also known as McDonald's most successful overseas development.

Another successful case is Seven-Eleven Japan Co., Ltd., which is in fact not actually a foreign company because Japan's well-known supermarket chain Ito-Yokado Co., Ltd. owns more than 50 percent of the shares in Seven-

て傘下に収めました。

ここ数年、アメリカのおもちゃ専門店チェーン、トイザらスをはじめ流通分野の外資企業の進出が相次ぎ、いずれも成功しています。ビッグバンを機に金融機関も日本への攻勢を強めるなど、最近は「第二の開国」といわれるほど外資系企業の進出ラッシュが続いています。

• **48**

Question | **外国企業の傘下に入った日本企業はありますか？**

Answer | いくつかありますが、その中で最大の企業は、ロータリーエンジンで有名な日本で5位の自動車メーカー、マツダです。

マツダは1980年代からアメリカのフォードと提携していましたが、輸出低迷と国内販売の不振で赤字に陥ったことから自力での再建を断念、96年、経営権をフォードに譲り、実質的にフォードの傘下に入りました。

フォードは、出資比率を24.5％から33.4％に引き上げるととともにヘンリー・ウォレス氏やジェームズ・ミラー氏を次々に社長として

Eleven Japan. Due to its success Seven-Eleven Japan bought South Land Ltd. in the United States, Seven-Eleven's parent company, making the company its affiliate.

Over the last few years specialist American retailers such as Toys 'R' Us and companies in the distribution business have started to advance into Japan one after another; many have been successful. Financial companies are using the opportunity of the Big Bang financial reforms to strengthen their offensive in Japan. The continuing rush of foreign firms into Japan is currently so intense that some people call it the second opening of Japan, *daini-no-kaikoku*.

• 48

Q: Are there Japanese companies that have become subsidiaries of foreign companies?

A: There are in fact several Japanese companies that have become subsidiaries of foreign corporations of which the most famous is Mazda Motor Corp., the number five automobile manufacturer in Japan, well-known for its rotary engines.

Since the 1980s, it has had a tie up with the American automobile manufacturer Ford. Low exports and a slump in domestic sales led to losses which made Mazda abandon its plans to try and rebuild itself into an internationally competitive manufacturer. In 1996 Ford "inherited" management control and in reality Mazda became a Ford subsidiary.

Ford increased its holdings in the company from 24.5 percent to 33.4 percent and Henry Wallace and subsequently James Miller became presidents of the company

送り込み、経営建て直しに当たっています。外国企業の傘下に入っても社長は日本人が務めるケースが多いのですが、マツダの場合、もう日本人に経営は任せておけないというフォードの判断があったようです。

　自動車メーカーでは、トラックの生産台数では世界1位を誇るいすゞ自動車もゼネラル・モーターズ（GM）の傘下に入っています。

　電機業界では、中堅の音響・映像機器メーカーの赤井電機と、やはり音響・映像機器メーカーの山水電気が、国内のオーディオ不況で経営が悪化したのを機に香港のセミ・テックグループに買収されました。現在はセミ・テックグループの支援で経営再建中です。

　精錬工場を持つ日本で唯一のアルミ一貫メーカーの日本軽金属は、カナダのアルミメーカー、アルキャン・アルミニウムの傘下に入っています。

• **49**

Question　**日本で株式を公開するにはどうしたらよいのですか？**

Answer　方法は二つあります。一つは全国8ヵ所にある証券取引所に株式を上場する方法です。もう一つはアメリカのNASDAQに相当する「店頭市場」に登録する方法です。どちらも基準があり、公開するにはこの基準をクリアしなければなりませんが、店頭市場の方が緩やかです。

and corporate restructuring began. There are many cases of Japanese individuals holding the position of president in subsidiaries of foreign companies in Japan but in the case of Mazda, Ford decided not to entrust management of the company to a Japanese.

The automobile manufacturer Isuzu Motors Ltd. which is proud of being the world's largest producer of trucks has become a subsidiary of General Motors Corp., an American manufacturer.

In the audio-visual equipment manufacturing industry, Akai Electric Co., Ltd. and Sansui Electric Co., Ltd. were badly hit by the downturn in the Japanese audio market and were takenover by a Hong Kong company, Semi-Tech Co., Ltd. Currently the companies are being rebuilt with financial assistance from Semi-Tech.

Japan's only integrated aluminum manufacturer with its own refinery, Nippon Light Metal Co., Ltd. is a subsidiary of the Canadian aluminum manufacturer Alcan Aluminum Ltd.

• **49**

Q: How do companies go public in Japan?

A: There are two routes. One is to float a company's shares on one of Japan's eight stock exchanges. The other is to register shares on the over-the-counter market, which is similar to NASDAQ in the United States. Both are regulated and no matter on which market shares are made public, regulatory hurdles have to be cleared. Needless to say, regulations of

　このためまず店頭市場で公開して実績を積んでから証券取引所の第2部に上場、さらに業績が拡大してくれば第1部に移行するというパターンが一般的です。

　例外もあり、NTTや日本たばこ産業、JR東日本などの民営化企業や三菱自動車工業、オリエンタルランド、フジテレビジョンをはじめとする大企業はいきなり第1部に上場しました。ソフトバンクも店頭公開してからわずか3年半後の98年1月、1部に直行上場しました。

　公開の基準は株式数や浮動株比率、株主数、株主資本の額、設立年数、配当や利益水準などです。店頭市場で公開するには日本証券業協会に登録するので基準は全国一律ですが、上場の場合は各取引所によって異なり、東京証券取引所が最も厳しく、他の取引所は緩めです。最近はベンチャー企業の育成や既存企業の活性化のため基準は緩和されてきています。

　98年現在の東証の基準は株式数は400万株以上、設立後3年以上で株主資本は10億円以上、配当は1株当たり年間5円以上などとなっています。基準を満たした企業は、日本証券業協会や証券取引所に申請、審査を受けます。いったん公開しても基準を満たさなくなれば登

the over-the-counter market are less stringent.

The usual pattern for companies in Japan is to initially go public on the over-the-counter market and then move to the second section of the stock exchange, once a good track record has been built. And finally move to the first section of the stock exchange if the business expands further.

However, there are exceptions. Some major corporations such as the privatized state-owned monopolies like Nippon Telegraph and Telephone Corp. (NTT), Japan Tobacco Inc. (JT) and East Japan Railway Co. as well as Mitsubishi Motors Corp., Oriental Land Co., Ltd., and Fuji Television Network Inc. leapt straight into the first section of the stock exchange on floatation. Softbank Corp. jumped directly to the first section after only spending three and a half years on the over-the-counter market.

Regulations concerning public offerings of stocks relate to the number of shares, the ratio of shares floated, the number of shareholders, the amount of shareholder capital, the number of years since the company was founded, and dividend and profit levels. Taking shares public on the over-the-counter market requires registration at the Japan Securities Dealers Association (JSDA). Regulations are uniform throughout Japan. But when it comes to floatations, each stock exchange has quite different regulations. The Tokyo Stock Exchange is the strictest while others are more lenient.

Recently, in an effort to invigorate venture businesses and help already established businesses, regulations are being eased. As of 1998, the regulations at the Tokyo Stock Exchange require companies to have more than 4 million shares, to have been established for at least three years, to have shareholder capital of more than 1 billion yen and to pay

録や上場は取り消されます。

3市場の上場会社と店頭公開会社数 (98年8月31日現在)

東京	1部	1334社	2部	485社
大阪	1部	878社	2部	395社
名古屋	1部	442社	2部	139社
店頭公開企業		862社		

・50

Question　**日本に有力なベンチャー・キャピタルはありますか?**

Answer　日本で最大のベンチャー・キャピタル(VC)は野村証券系のジャフコです。同社は株式会社組織で、株式は店頭登録しており、1000億円を超える自己資金を持っています。97年度は239社に総額約380億円を投資しました。

　そのほかの有力VCとしては、日本インベストメント・ファイナンスや日本アジア投資など銀行や証券、保険会社系など150を超えるVCがあります。

　日本のVCの場合、資金の出し手は金融機関や一般企業で、いまは不況で資金がなかなか集まりません。しかも投資先のベンチャー企業の倒産もこのところ増えています。
　このため各VCとも投資には慎重になっています。株式公開のめどが立った安全な企業に

more than 5 yen in dividends per share. Companies that satisfy these various conditions apply to JSDA or the various stock exchanges and have their application vetted. If they fail to meet these regulations even after going public their registration or shares will be removed from the markets.

• 50

Q: Are there influential venture capitalists in Japan?

A: In Japan the largest venture capital (VC) firm is Jafco Co., Ltd., a Nomura Securities Co., Ltd. affiliate, joint stock company registered on the over-the-counter-market. It has 100 billion yen of its own investment capital. In 1997, it had investments in 239 companies totalling 38 billion yen.

In addition to Jafco there are other influential venture capital firms including Japan Investment Finance and Japan-Asia Investments. In Japan there are more than 150 venture capital companies. Many are affiliated to banks, security houses and insurance companies.

VCs in Japan usually invest funds on behalf of companies and financial organizations. The current recession has made it very difficult to collect funds and recently the number of venture businesses going bankrupt has been increasing.

Japanese VCs are very prudent about their investments. There is a strong trend only to invest in companies that are

投資する傾向が強く、出来立てほやほやでリスクの高い本当のベンチャー企業に投資するVCはあまりありません。

各VCの投資先をみても、設立後10年以上のベンチャー企業への投資額が半分を超えており、設立5年未満の企業への投資は20%にも達していません。このへんにも日本でベンチャービジネスが育たない一因があるようです。

最近はようやくコンピューターやエレクトロニクスなどハイテク業種を中心に設立後間もない若い企業に投資、育成しようという傾向が出始めていますが、ベンチャー企業の本格的な育成にはまだ力不足といわざるを得ません。

・51

Question｜**日本にシンクタンクはありますか？**

Answer｜日本には約500のシンクタンクがあります。数は多いのですが、銀行や証券などの系列下にあり、独立系のシンクタンクが多いアメリカとは社会における役割も大きく異なっています。

アメリカのシンクタンクは、さまざまな政策課題について独自の案を提言、世論を動かすなど国の政策遂行にも影響を与えています。これに比べて日本のシンクタンクの大半は営

viewed as safe and have already put together plans to make their shares public. There is almost no investment by VCs in Japan in fresh, newly established high-risk companies, which are in the true sense venture businesses.

Looking at investments by Japanese VCs, half of all their investments are in venture companies that were established more than 10 years ago. Investments in companies that have been around for less than ten years do not even reach 20 percent of total investments. This is one of the reasons why it has been difficult to develop venture businesses in Japan.

However, recently a new trend of investing in and trying to nurture young, newly established companies in computer and electronics related high-technology industries has finally started. But the encouragement of real venture businesses in Japan is still desperately inadequate.

• 51

Q: Do think-tanks exist in Japan?

A: In Japan there are about 500 think-tanks. They are large in number but are usually affiliated to banks and stockbrokers. The situation in Japan is significantly different from the United States, where there are many independent think-tanks that play important roles in society.

Think-tanks in the United States develop independent proposals for policy issues and play influential roles in moving public opinion and in the execution of government policy. However, the vast majority of Japanese think-tanks are profit-

利企業で、企業からの受託調査により収入を得ているという制約があり、収入につながらない政策提言をする余裕はありません。

こうしたシンクタンクは「頭脳集団」というより、企業の下請け調査機関といった方が正確かもしれません。しかも全体の約70%は、研究員が20人未満の小規模シンクタンクで、研究分野も国土開発、産業分析、マクロ経済などに偏っており、環境問題や国際・外交分野の研究は手薄です。

非営利のシンクタンクもありますが、こちらも政府から補助金をもらったりしているので、国の政策を批判するようなことはできず、調査が主体です。

背景には、官僚が政策情報を独占して離さないという事情もあります。官僚主導の政策運営は行き詰まっており、国民各層の意見を反映するよう、多様な提案、提言がいまの日本には必要なのですが、残念ながら日本のシンクタンクはそうした提言をして世論を動かしていく力はありません。

代表的なシンクタンク

三菱総合研究所	三菱グループ系の日本の代表的なシンクタンク
総合研究開発機構	政府系の政策志向型シンクタンク
野村総合研究所	野村証券系の総合シンクタンク
日本総合研究所	住友銀行系の総合シンクタンク
国民経済研究所	マクロ経済に強いシンクタンク
社会経済生産性本部	年金、雇用、賃金などの研究に定評のあるシンクタンク
ロシア東欧貿易会	ロシア・東欧諸国の経済分析に強いシンクタンク

making entities earning income from contracts with companies who have entrusted them to conduct surveys on their behalf. These think-tanks do not have the time to make policy proposals that will not earn them revenue.

More than being think-tanks these organizations are probably more accurately described as company affiliated research organizations. About 70 percent of all Japanese think-tanks are small in scale and employ fewer than 20 researchers. The fields of research they lean towards include real estate development, industrial analysis, and macroeconomics. Environmental issues and international diplomacy are generally not given a high priority and are poorly staffed.

Not-for-profit think-tanks do exist in Japan but they are financially supported by the government and are unable to criticize official government policy. The majority of their work consists of conducting surveys.

Government officials monopolize policy information and are unable to sever their links from the policies they administer. Execution and development of government policy by bureaucrats often ends in deadlock and despite their need, proposals that truly reflect the opinions of all the different layers of Japanese society are non-existent. Unfortunately, in Japan think-tanks do not have the ability to mobilize public opinion.

・52

<table>
<tr><td>**Q**uestion</td><td>**日本では外国企業に対する規制はありますか？**</td></tr>
<tr><td>**A**nswer</td><td>以前は国内企業保護のため、外国企業は100％出資子会社を設立できないなど厳しい規制がありました。しかし、いまは外国企業だけを対象とした規制はほとんどなくなり、国内企業も外国企業も同じ条件で競争するようになりました。

　日本ではそもそもビジネスに対する政府の規制が多すぎるのが問題で、バブル後の不況でようやく政府も重い腰を上げ、産業のさまざまな分野の規制緩和や構造改革に取り組むようになりました。金融ビッグバンもその一環です。

　それでもまだ外国企業は、日本の規制に大きな不満を感じているようです。不満は①世界に通用しない基準を押しつける　②基準そのものが曖昧　③手続きが複雑－などが代表的なものです。

　こうした不満は日本企業も感じているのですが、日本企業がいくら声をあげても改まらず、外国企業が自国政府を通じて要求すると緩和されることが結構あります。日本政府は「外圧」に弱いからで、外圧による規制緩和で結果的に恩恵を受けるのは日本企業というケースもあります。</td></tr>
</table>

• 52

Q: In Japan are there special regulations uniquely for foreign companies?

A: Previously, strict regulations existed in order to protect Japanese companies that prohibited overseas corporations from setting up 100 percent owned local subsidiaries in Japan. But now almost all regulations aimed uniquely at overseas companies have disappeared, allowing overseas companies to compete on a level playing field with local Japanese companies.

Nevertheless, the over regulation of business by government has become a major problem. The Japanese government finally started easing its position on deregulation during the recession following the collapse of the bubble economy. The government is now dealing with this by easing regulations in various industries and grappling with structural reforms. The Big Bang financial deregulations are part of this process.

Despite this, overseas companies are still dissatisfied with Japanese regulations. Typical complaints include Japan pushing standards that are not valid internationally, standards that are vague and obscure, and application procedures that are too complex.

Japanese companies also have similar complaints but no matter how often they object there never seems to be any improvement. On the other hand, non-Japanese companies are able to raise their demands through their respective governments and many times this has actually led to an easing of regulations. The Japanese government is strongly influenced

政府や自治体の規制だけでなく、日本のビジネス界のルールも外国企業は参入障壁と感じているようです。代表例は業界団体です。日本では業界の利益を守るためあらゆる業界が団体を作っていますが、外国企業の加入はなかなか認められず、外国企業は情報の入手などで苦労しているようです。

• 53

Question   最も成長著しい産業分野はどこですか？

Answer   いまは通信を中心にした情報産業です。日本でインターネット接続の商用サービスが始まったのは93年ですが、プロバイダーは97年には全国で2000社にも達しました。過当競争も目立っており、廃業に追い込まれる業者も相次いでいるほどです。

携帯電話の加入者も爆発的に増えています。98年7月末には約3500万台に達し、国民の4人に1人以上が携帯電話を利用している計算になりますが、まだまだ増えそうです。

企業のリストラ進行とともに人材派遣業も急成長しています。成人を対象とするカルチ

by *gaiatsu*, foreign or overseas pressure. In some cases the easing of regulations following *gaiatsu* has actually ended up being more beneficial for Japanese companies.

It is not just the regulations drawn up by central and local government but also the "rules" which govern the world of Japanese business which are seen by many foreign companies as fences erected in their paths. A typical example is Japanese trade organizations. In order to protect profitability, in almost all industries Japanese companies set up trade organizations. It is often very difficult for foreign companies to join these organizations and many struggle to gain information about their activities including self-regulation.

• 53

Q: What are the fastest growing business sectors in Japan?

A: Telecommunications centered around information based industries is the fastest growing business sector in Japan. The first commercial internet access provider was set up in Japan in 1993. But by 1997, there were 2,000 providers throughout Japan. Excessive competition now exists and one provider after another has been pushed out of business.

The number of people using cellular telephones has exploded. By the end of July 1998, the number had reached about 35 million, with one in four people in Japan using cellular telephones, and the number is expected to increase further.

The increase of companies restructuring their operations has led to a rapid growth in the number of employment agen-

ャースクールなども含めた教育産業も引き続き有望です。ガーデニングブームで園芸関係の市場も急拡大、環境マインドの高まりで、省エネなど環境関連市場も膨らんでいます。

　しかし、日本の将来の最有望市場は何と言ってもシルバー産業でしょう。日本では2015年には国民の4人に1人が65歳以上という超高齢社会を迎えます。このためさまざまな高齢者向けの商品がすでに開発されています。

　住宅会社は、段差のない浴室やエレベーター付きの3階建て住宅を売り出し、家電業界は高齢者にも使いやすい洗濯機や冷蔵庫などを開発しています。旅行会社は、ゆったりした日程の高齢者用パック旅行の扱いを始めました。老人ホームやホームヘルパーなど介護関連産業も成長が予想され、商社やメーカーなどさまざまな業種の企業が参入しようとしています。

成長が期待される分野の国内市場

	1993年	2000年	2010年
情報通信関連	6兆円	87兆円	155兆円
企業活動支援関連	18兆円	32兆円	55兆円
医療保険・福祉関連	37兆円	55兆円	69兆円
余暇・生活関連	38兆円	61兆円	92兆円
環境関連	12兆円	18兆円	24兆円

（注）経済企画庁の試算

cies. The improving business environment for adult education schools including culture training, continues unabated. The Japanese gardening boom has rapidly expanded the market for horticulture related products. Increased awareness about the environment has swelled the market for environment related and energy saving products.

But the industry which has the best prospects of all in Japan is the "silver industry" or senior citizens industry. Japan faces the prospect of a rapidly ageing society. By 2015 one in four Japanese will be over the age of 65. With this new market in mind, various different new products and services are already being developed.

Real estate developers are building bathrooms without steps and with flat floors and selling three story residential houses with elevators. Household appliance makers are developing washing machines and refrigerators that are easy for the aged to use. Travel agents have started package tours for senior citizens with easy-going schedules. Old age homes, home helpers and other care related industries are expected to grow and trading companies, manufacturers and companies from various other industries are gearing up to participate in this expanding business area.

・54

Question | 日本の通信販売業界の現状は？

Answer | 日本の通信販売業界は、安さを武器に1980年代以降急成長を続けてきましたが、最近は伸びも止まり、業界として曲がり角に来ています。

背景には、大手の量販店が価格破壊で恒常的に値引きをするようになり、通信販売の割安感が薄れたことに加え、顧客層として想定していた20代から40代の女性の開拓が一段落したことがあります。テレビショッピングが伸びていることも一因です。

衣料・生活関連の通信販売トップ、セシールの98年3月期の売上高は減収となり、他の通信販売会社も軒並み売上高が減っています。この結果、全国で約280社に上る通信販売業界全体の売上高は97年度は約2兆2000億円と96年度に比べ、わずかながら減少しました。

日本では高齢者や中年男性で通信販売を利用する人はあまりいません。しかし、高齢者にとって通信販売は便利な手段です。高齢社会に向けて高齢者向けのサービスを強化するなど新たな市場を開拓すれば、業界は再び成長軌道に乗ることができるかもしれません。

• 54

Q: How are mail order catalogue businesses doing in Japan?

A: Since the 1980s, mail order companies in Japan utilizing low prices to sell goods have grown in a consistent and rapid way. But more recently this growth has tapered off, leaving the industry at a turning point.

Large Japanese retailers have constantly been offering discounts in what has become known as "price destruction" eroding the inexpensive image of mail order goods. In addition, the customer segments that mail order companies have been targeting and trying to develop, women in their 20s to 40s, has recently stopped expanding. Another factor affecting the industry is the increased popularity of television shopping.

In March 1998, the turnover of the top mail order company, Cécile Co., ltd. which sells clothes and household goods, fell. Other mail order companies in Japan also saw their turnover fall resulting in an overall drop for the approximately 280 mail order companies in 1997 to 2 trillion 200 billion yen, a small decrease on 1996.

Currently, in Japan very few elderly or middle-aged men use mail order catalogues, despite the fact that ordering goods from mail order catalogues is extremely convenient for old people. As the Japanese population continues to age companies that strengthen services directed at the aged will be able to develop new markets for their services. The industry may even be able to return to its former path of rapid growth.

• **55**

| **Question** | 日本の流行の発信地はどこですか？ |

| **Answer** | 日本の若者消費、流行は女子高生がリードしています。新しい物好きで購買意欲が旺盛だからです。大手マーケティング会社の担当者も女子高生の消費行動を常にウオッチしています。消費者モニターとして女子高生と専属契約している企業もあるほどです。
「たまごっち」も、試作品を女子高生らに見せたら評判になり、世界的なブームになりました。女子高生が集まる流行の最先端を行く街は東京の渋谷です。原宿とともに全国の女子高生にとって一度は行きたい「聖地」と見られています。

　聖地を闊歩する女子高生の人気商品ベストスリーは、ケータイ（携帯電話）、ピッチ（PHS）、プリクラ（プリント倶楽部）。使い捨てカメラやジーンズのビンテージ復刻版、ブランド服なども人気があります。ポケベル、ルーズソックスなどはやや下火です。
　高校生ですからアルバイトをしても使える小遣いは限られています。ケータイやピッチの通話料がかさむ分、カラオケからは足が遠のいているようで、カラオケボックスはどこも青息吐息の状態です。 |

• 55

Q: Where do Japanese consumer fashions and crazes start?

A: Japanese high school girls, with a love for and a strong desire to purchase new things, lead youth consumer fashions. Executives at large marketing companies watch purchasing patterns of high school girls carefully and some even sign up high school girls on exclusive contracts to monitor and test new products.

Trial products of Tamagotchi (cyber or virtual pets) shown to high school girls were greeted enthusiastically and ended up being a worldwide hit. High school girls like to meet in Shibuya, in Tokyo, an area which is now considered to have the cutting-edge for new Japanese fashions. Shibuya and Harajuku are the fashion meccas that high school girls from all over Japan want to visit at least once.

Currently, the top three products amongst high school girls strolling this holy ground are *keitai*, *picchi* and *purikura*, cell phones, digital personal-handy phones (PHS) and print clubs respectively. Disposable cameras, replica vintage jeans, and international designer brands are also popular. But pagers and long socks are already out.

As they are just high school students, even if they have part-time jobs, their pocket money is limited. The telephone charges on cell phones and PHSs mount up and have created a financial barrier between them and *karaoke* parlors, yesterday's fashion. *Karaoke* parlors, wherever they are in

　　女子高生は夢中になるのも早いが、醒める
のも早いので目が離せません。しかも最近は
消費のリード役が女子中学生へとますます低
年齢化する傾向があります。いずれ小学生が
リード役になる時代が来るかも知れません。

• **56**

Question　**日本にヘッジファンドはありますか？**

Answer　ジョージ・ソロスの「クォンタム・ファンド」や
ジュリアン・ロバートソンの「タイガー・ファ
ンド」のような大型ヘッジファンドは、残念な
がら日本にはありません。大富豪など少数の投
資家から資金を預かり運用する、海外のヘッ
ジファンドのマネジャーたちからは、日本の
金融市場は草刈り場とみられているようです。
　　しかし、日本もいよいよビッグバンに突入、
海外のヘッジファンドの活動を指をくわえて
みているわけにはいかない、とばかりに和製
ヘッジファンドもぼちぼち誕生しています。
　　アメリカの有力ファンドで修行した日本人
ファンドマネジャーらが設立したものです。
資産規模はまだ小さく、国際金融市場で相場
を動かすような力はありませんが、いずれは
世界のビッグプレーヤーを目指しています。
　　日本でも明治から昭和にかけて株の世界で

Japan, have now hit hard times.

High school girls become obsessed quickly but are also extremely fickle and move on to the next fad just as quickly. Their tastes and interests have to be monitored carefully. But recently junior high school girls are leading the crazes and the tendency seems to be for the trend setters to get younger. In due course it will no doubt be Japanese primary school pupils who play the leading trend setting role.

• 56

Q: Do hedge funds exist in Japan?

A: Unfortunately, large hedge funds like George Soros's Quantum Fund and Julian Robertson's Tiger Fund do not exist in Japan. Japan's financial markets currently offer rich pickings for foreign hedge fund mangers who look after and invest funds on behalf of small numbers of extremely wealthy investors.

But as Japan's Big Bang financial reforms approach, foreign hedge funds should not just be looked at covetously. Japanese hedge funds are slowly coming into existence.

They are being set up by Japanese managers who have worked and trained at leading American hedge funds. The scale of their capital is currently small and they do not have the ability to move international markets. Nevertheless, they are intent on becoming big global players.

Between the Meiji (1868–1912) and Showa (1926–1989)

は有名な相場師がいました。日露戦争（1904-5年）当時活躍した鈴木久五郎や、同じく明治期に名うての相場師といわれた野村証券の創業者の野村徳七、昭和に入ってからは鐘紡株買いで失敗、自殺した太田収らです。

　最近は先物取引をはじめとするデリバティブ（金融派生商品）を使い、相場の舞台は株から通貨、金利、債券などへと大きく広がっています。ビッグバンをきっかけに日本のヘッジファンドのファンドマネジャーが日本だけでなく、世界のビッグプレーヤーとして認められる可能性もあります。

periods there were several famous Japanese speculators. Kyugoro Suzuki who was active during the Russo-Japan War (1904–1905) became a renowned *sobashi*, speculator, as did Tokushichi Nomura, the founder of Nomura Securities, during the Meiji Period. In the Showa Period, Osamu Ota was famous but he committed suicide after making huge losses trying to corner the market in shares in Kanebo, Ltd.

Recently, the use of financial derivatives such as futures and options in shares, currencies, interest rates and bonds has increased widely. Japan's Big Bang financial reforms could be the catalyst for Japan's hedge fund managers to gain international recognition as big global players.

日本のサラリーマン
PART 1

Working in Corporate Japan: The *Salaryman*
PART 1

• **57**

Question｜**平均的なサラリーマンの収入と暮らし向きは？**

Answer｜国税庁によると、民間企業に勤めるサラリーマンやＯＬの96年1年間の平均給与は461万円。男女別では男性が569万円、女性が276万円と男性は女性の2倍以上です。これはあくまで統計上の数値で、東京の大企業に勤める大卒40歳のサラリーマンのごく平均的な暮らし向きは、次のような感じになります。

　年収は企業によってばらつきがあり、800万円程度から1200万円程度。小学生の子供2人の4人家族で、妻は専業主婦かパートタイマー。延べ床面積70m²から120m²ほどの郊外の一戸建て住宅か、マンションに住み、一戸建ての場合、イヌやネコを飼うケースが多い。

　2000万円ぐらいの住宅ローンを抱え、ローンの支払いと塾代など子供の教育費に追われている。朝は7時半ごろ家を出て満員電車に1時間から1時間半ほど揺られ、9時前に会社に到着。仕事の後、週に1、2回は会社近くの居酒屋やバーで同僚と軽く一杯、たまに2次会でカラオケになることも。

• 57

Q: **What type of life and income does the average Japanese *salaryman* have?**

A: According to the National Tax Administration Agency, *salarymen* and office ladies (OLs) working in private companies have an average annual income of 4,610,000 yen. If you separate out men and women, men earn almost twice as much as women with an annual income of about 5,690,000 yen, compared with 2,760,000 yen for women.

An average 40-year-old *salaryman* working in Tokyo as a departmental director for a major Japanese company can expect to earn between 8 and 12 million yen per year, although annual earnings differ considerably from company to company. He will probably have two children in primary school making up a family unit of four. His wife will be a housewife or perhaps have a part-time job. He will probably live in a detached house or condominium in the suburbs of Tokyo of between 70 m^2 and 120 m^2 in size. If it is a house they will probably have a dog or cat as a pet.

He will probably have a mortgage of about 20 million yen and spend the rest of his money on cram schools and education for the children. He will leave home about 7.30 am each morning and have an hour, or an hour and a half, long commute to work in a packed train, arriving at work just before 9.00 am. On average he will go out for a quick drink twice a week at a pub near the office with his colleagues and may sometimes go on to a *karaoke* bar for a singsong.

　　週末は妻の買い物に付き合ったり、ファミリーレストランで食事をしたり、行楽地にドライブしたりして過ごします。2ヵ月に1回ぐらいの割で同僚とゴルフに行き、まとまった休みが取れるのは夏と正月に各1週間程度。その休みも帰省か、家でぶらぶらして過ごすうちに終わってしまいます。

• **58**

Question｜「過労死」はなぜ起きるのですか?

Answer｜日本人は海外から「ウサギ小屋に住む仕事狂」と揶揄されたことがありました。その後、住宅事情はやや改善され、残業時間も減っていますが、それでも働き過ぎで若いサラリーマンやOLが死ぬことがときどきあり、「過労死」として社会問題になっています。

　　働きすぎて病気になって死ぬ、というのは欧米でもたまに起きるでしょうが、日本の過労死はもっと激しく、長時間労働の末に突然死んだり、鬱状態に追い込まれて自殺するというケースです。

　　91年、大手広告代理店の24歳のサラリーマンが連日深夜に及ぶ長時間勤務の結果、自殺に追い込まれました。遺族の訴えに対し東京地方裁判所の裁判長は「常軌を逸した長時間労働が自殺の原因」として会社に約1億2000万

At the weekend he will probably go shopping with his wife and eat out at a family restaurant or perhaps take the family for a drive or an excursion. Once every couple of months he will join his work colleagues in a game of golf. The only times he will be able to take a few consecutive days leave will be in the summer or at new year for about a week, which he will probably spend visiting his home town or idling away at home.

• 58

Q: Why does *karoshi*, death through overwork, happen?

A: Japanese people have been mocked from overseas for being fanatical workers living in rabbit hutches. Housing has now improved and the number of hours of overtime worked has fallen. However, young salaried workers still die, occasionally, from overwork. *Karoshi*, death through overwork, has become a social problem.

Overwork leading to illness and death occasionally occurs in Europe and the United States as well. But Japan's *karoshi* problem is very severe with sudden death occurring after long hours of work and cases of depression leading to suicide.

In 1991, a 24-year-old employee of a major advertising company committed suicide after working long hours until midnight consecutively over a number of days. His family sued the company and the judge presiding over the case at the Tokyo district court ruled that the abnormally long hours

円の損害賠償金の支払いを命じる判決を出し、過労死が認められました。

　裁判などで過労死と認定されるのは氷山の一角です。過労が原因とみられても認定されず、自殺や「突然死」として扱われるケースは相当数に上るとみられます。

　日本では「仕事は人生を楽しむ手段」とか、「仕事は仕事、遊びは遊び」と割り切れずに、家庭や自分の健康を犠牲にしてまで働く「会社人間」が大勢います。会社人間になりたくなくても、そうならざるを得ない雰囲気が日本の一部の会社にはあります。有給休暇でさえ自由に取れない会社が多いのです。

　背景には休むことへの罪悪感と、休む人を快く思わない風土があります。こうした風土が変わらない限り、日本のサラリーマン社会から過労死をなくすのは難しいでしょう。

・59

Question｜日本では今も終身雇用制は存在しますか？

Answer｜学校を卒業してすぐに就職した企業に定年まで勤める「終身雇用制」は、日本の高度経済成長の秘密、と高く評価された時期もありました。社員はクビの心配をしないで働けるた

of work were the cause of suicide. The court reached a verdict recognizing the cause of death as *karoshi* and ordered the company to pay 120 million yen in compensation.

Cases of *karoshi* recognized by the courts are probably just the tip of the iceberg. There are thought to be many cases of death through overwork that are not recognized as such and are treated as suicide, or death through natural causes.

It is often said that "work is a means towards enjoying life" and "work is work and play is play" but in reality in Japan many people cannot separate the two. They often work until their family life and health are sacrificed. Even if one does not want to devote oneself totally to the company, in Japan many organizations have a corporate atmosphere that makes it almost unavoidable.

At many companies it is not easy to take paid leave despite being owed leave. This makes taking paid leave feel like a crime and creates a climate where people who take time off are viewed unfavorably by their colleagues and managers. Unless the corporate climate changes it will be difficult to erase *karoshi* from Japanese society.

• 59

Q: Does Japan's lifetime employment system still exist?

A: Japan's lifetime employment system, which enabled people to join a company straight after graduating from university and to remain at the same company until retirement, was at one point highly admired internationally. It was often

め、会社に対する忠誠心が高まり、高い生産
性につながるとみられたからです。

　しかし、いまや終身雇用制は過去のものに
なりつつあります。転職するサラリーマンが
増える一方、低成長への移行で企業にとって
定年まで雇用を保証するのがだんだん難しく
なってきているからです。

　リストラの対象となり、肩たたきを受けて
退職を余儀なくされたり、子会社や関係会社
への移籍を命じられるなど40代、50代になる
と、最初に入った会社に残れる人は年々少な
くなっています。終身雇用制は近い将来、日
本でも「死語」になる可能性があります。

　終身雇用制の崩壊とともに退職金制度見直
しの動きも出ています。日本企業の退職金は
定年まで勤め上げた社員に支給することを原
則にしています。そのため金額は勤務年数に
応じて累増する仕組みになっている企業が多
く、定年まで勤めれば大企業の場合2000万円
から3000万円の退職金をもらえますが、若く
して退職すると不利になります。

　松下電器産業は、退職するときに退職金を
受け取るか、それとも退職金分を月々の給料
に上乗せして先に受け取るかを社員が選択で
きる制度を導入しました。これだと転職して
も不利になりません。終身雇用を最初から前

cited as the secret behind Japan's high economic growth rates. Employees working in an environment free from worries about job losses were thought to be more devoted to the corporation employing them, which increased productivity.

However, now lifetime employment is increasingly becoming something of the past. The number of *salarymen* changing jobs continues to rise and it is becoming increasingly difficult for Japanese corporations with low growth rates to guarantee employment for their staff until retirement.

Corporate down-sizing and retiring after receiving the proverbial *katatataki* "the tap on the shoulder" are now unavoidable. Being ordered to transfer to affiliated companies is more and more common amongst people in their 40s and 50s and every year there are fewer people who remain as employees of the companies they originally joined. In the future, lifetime employment may become a redundant expression.

With the end of lifetime employment the current system of paying one-off retirement allowances to employees is also under reconsideration. The principle behind Japan's retirement allowance system is that the employee works at the same company right up to retirement. Many Japanese companies calculate the retirement allowance based on the number of years worked; if one works up to retirement age major companies pay one-off retirement allowances of between 20 million to 30 million yen. People who retire early or when they are young are at a great disadvantage.

Matsushita Electric Industrial Co., Ltd. recently introduced a system which allows employees to opt to receive the retirement allowance when they retire or the equivalent sum as an extra monthly payment added to their salary. Under this system, one is not penalized if one changes jobs. Other

・**60**

Question 日本で在宅勤務は普及していますか？

Answer 在宅勤務は通勤ラッシュの解消になり、障害者の雇用確保にもつながるとして政府は普及を推進していますが、自宅や、自宅近くのサテライトオフィスで仕事をしている「テレワーク」人口は、現在まだ約100万人、全就業者の中の1.5%程度で、アメリカに比べると普及はかなり遅れています。

　大企業でも在宅勤務を導入するところがぼちぼち出てきていますが、在宅勤務者で多いのは、脱サラして独立した人や子育て中の主婦らです。ある調査では、在宅勤務者の約3分の2が女性で、請負自営の独立型が83%、残り17%が副業型と社員型で、なかでも独立型の半数は子供のいる女性でした。

　在宅勤務は、通勤がないというメリットはありますが、仕事の確保の難しさと収入の低さが悩みの種です、週に60時間以上働いても30%近くの人の年収は300万円にも達しておらず、平均的なサラリーマンの半分以下です。

companies are showing interest in the scheme as it is not based on the initial premise of employing someone for life.

• 60

Q: Is telecommuting and working from home on the increase in Japan?

A: The Japanese government is trying to encourage working from home as it reduces the rush hour commuter crush and helps secure employment for disabled people. But the number of telecommuters working from home or from satellite offices near their homes is still only around 1 million people, about 1.5 percent of the total working population of Japan. Compared to the United States the spread in Japan has been slow.

Large Japanese companies occasionally introduce schemes for working from home but the majority of people who do this have decided to leave the corporate world behind and work independently or are housewives raising children. According to one survey two thirds of people working from home are women, of which 83 percent are self-employed. The remaining 17 percent work for companies or are conducting side businesses. Half of those working independently are women with children.

Working from home has the merit of being able to avoid the daily commuter rush but it does not provide job security and is distressingly low paid. Even working more than 60 hours a week only guarantees 30 percent of people a salary of less than 3 million yen a year. This is less than half the

自宅でラクに仕事をして高収入とはいかない
ようです。

　アメリカなどに比べ日本の在宅勤務者の待
遇が悪い背景には、通信費など経費の高さに
加え、個人より組織を重視する日本独特の社
会風土があります。弁護士や会計士など資格
を持っている人は別にして、一般的に組織に
属さない個人はあまり信用されず、いい仕事
もなかなか得られません。

• 61

Question　**サラリーマンが頻繁に名刺を交換する
のはなぜですか？**

Answer　印刷された名刺を交換する習慣は、明治時代
以降、ヨーロッパやアメリカから日本に入っ
てきたのですが、今では日本のビジネスマン
が世界で最も頻繁に名刺を交換しているので
はないでしょうか。

　名刺には肩書きや電話番号、最近はEメー
ルのアドレスなども書いてあり、連絡などの
際に非常に便利なので、初対面のビジネスマ
ンは必ず名刺を交換します。名刺はビジネス
マンの必需品で、会社は新入社員に何はとも
あれ名刺を支給します。

　これほど普及した理由の一つは、日本語の
漢字にあるのではないでしょうか。日本人の

amount an average *salaryman* is paid. Working comfortably at home on a high salary in Japan seems almost unachievable.

Compared with the United States and other countries general conditions for people who work from home are poor. In addition to high communication costs there is the peculiar Japanese characteristic of regarding companies as more important than individuals. With the exception of qualified lawyers and accountants, individuals who do not belong to any organization are less trusted or respected and find it difficult to find interesting work.

• 61

Q: Why do Japanese businessmen exchange business cards so frequently?

A: The habit of exchanging *meishi,* business cards, began in the Meiji Period when the idea was imported from Europe and the United States. But now Japanese businessmen probably exchange more business cards a year than anyone else in the world.

On printed cards, job titles, telephone numbers and more recently e-mail addresses and other items are written. As they are extremely useful when wanting to get in contact with someone, businessmen always exchange cards when they meet for the first time. Business cards are essential equipment for Japanese businessmen and new employees at companies are supplied with them before anything else.

One of the reasons why their usage has spread to the extent it has is probably because of the *kanji* characters

名前は、発音は同じでも字が違う場合が結構あります。例えば姓の場合、「イトウ」は伊藤、伊東、井藤など、「ナガシマ」には永島、長島、長嶋などがあります。名前の場合は、同音でもっと多くの表記があります。例えば「アキラ」ですと昭、明、章、亮、晃、輝、晶、昌…などキリがないくらいです。

　口頭で名乗る場合、字を説明しなければなりませんが、「長島昭」と書いてある名刺を渡せばその説明もいらず、もらった方も字を確認する必要はありません。

　名刺の交換にもマナーがあります。年下、目下の人が先に出すのがエチケット。貰った後は、丁寧に名刺入れにしまうか、商談の際などはしばらくテーブルの上に置き、肩書きや名前を頭に入れた後にさりげなく名刺入れにしまうやり方が普通です。相手の名刺をぞんざいに扱ったり、メモ用紙代わりに使ったりするは厳禁です。

(Chinese ideograms) that are used in Japanese. There are many cases of Japanese names with the same pronunciation being written using different *kanji* characters. For example, Ito can be written in the following ways: 伊藤, 伊東, 井藤. Nagashima can be written: 永島, 長島, 長嶋. With first names there are even more ways of writing names with the same pronunciation. For example, the many different ways the name Akira can be written are almost endless including: 昭, 明, 章, 亮, 晃, 輝, 晶, 昌.

If you introduce yourself verbally you have to explain the characters used to write your name but if you hand over a business card with Akira Nagashima written on it there is no need to explain and the person receiving the card does not need to confirm the *kanji* characters used in your name.

There is an etiquette to exchanging business cards. The younger, junior person should hand over his card first. On receipt the business card should be put carefully into a business card holder or placed on the table during discussions. Once names and titles have been memorized it is usual for people to put the cards into their business card holders. Using someone's business card in a carefree manner or to jot down notes on is strictly forbidden.

• **62**

Question　年俸制の導入は進んでいますか？

Answer　日本企業の賃金は、社員の勤続年数や年齢とともに基本給が上がる「年功制」が基本でしたが、個人の能力や成績をもっと賃金に反映させようと、働きぶりに応じて年間の給料総額を決める年俸制を導入する企業がじわじわと増えています。

　成績を上げた社員の賃金は増やし、成績の良くない社員の賃金は減らすことにより、人材の流動化に対応するとともに中高年社員の活性化を図るのが目的です。

　ソニーは日本企業では最も早く1969年に導入、現在、社員の4分の1の約5000人が年俸制の対象となっています。東京電力やトヨタ自動車、NTTなども一部の管理職、専門職を対象に導入しました。

　中央労働委員会が97年6月に実施した調査では、企業の18.5%がすでに年俸制を導入しており、9.9%が導入を予定しています。2001年には日本企業の4社に1社が導入するとの予想もあります。

　しかし、年俸制は、日本のほとんどの企業にとって初めての経験ですから、社員の間で

• 62

Q: Are annual salary schemes increasing in Japan?

A: Wages at Japanese companies increase on the basis of the number of years of service and age, in a system built around seniority. However, companies introducing annual salary schemes which base annual compensation on how hard people work are gradually increasing in an effort to make pay reflect an individual's ability and performance.

Employees who achieve good results receive salary increases and poorly performing employees have their salaries reduced under a system which is designed to mobilize staff and activate middle-aged workers.

In 1969 Sony Corp. was the first major company in Japan to introduce an annual salary scheme. Currently, one quarter of its staff, about 5,000 people, are now on annual salary schemes. The Tokyo Electric Power Co., Inc., Toyota Motor Corp., Nippon Telegraph and Telephone Corp. (NTT) and other major companies have also introduced similar schemes for some of their managers and technical experts.

According to a survey conducted by the Central Labor Relations Committee in June 1997, 18.9 percent of all companies have already introduced annual salary schemes and a further 9.9 percent of companies plan to do so. By 2001 one in four Japanese companies is expected to have introduced annual pay schemes. However, it is the first time for most companies to run annual pay schemes and it has left many

戸惑いもあります。各社とも試行錯誤しているのが実情で、まだ定着したとは言えません。

最大の問題は、能力や成績の評価方法です。人は普通、自分の能力を2割程度過大評価するといいますが、評価の結果、社員がやる気を出すこともあれば、逆にやる気を失うこともあるからです。

年俸制は世界的な流れですから日本企業も避けて通るわけにはいきません。試行錯誤しながらも年功制から年俸制へと徐々に移行していくことになりそうです。

• 63

Question　会社に学閥はありますか？

Answer　特定の一流大学の出身者を大量に採用する、その結果、役員や社長になるのも特定大学の出身者が多くなるというという意味で、「学閥」を形成している大学はあります。しかし、そうした大学は東京大学や慶應義塾大学などごく一部で、それ以外の日本に約600ある大学のほとんどは学閥とは無縁です。

東大閥として知られるのはＪＲ東日本、日本興業銀行、新日本製鉄、富士銀行、ファナ

members of staff bewildered. The reality is that many companies are running these schemes by trial and error and the new schemes cannot yet be said to have taken root.

The biggest problem is how to evaluate results and productivity. It is often said that people overexaggerate their ability by 20 percent. Evaluations can motivate staff but can also have the opposite effect of destroying their motivation.

Annual pay schemes are a worldwide phenomenon and there is now no way that Japanese companies can avoid introducing them. Japanese companies will no doubt continue to move slowly away from salaries based on seniority to annual pay schemes based on ability and productivity.

• 63

Q: Do *gakubatsu*, cliques of people from the same universities, exist within Japanese companies?

Q: The recruitment of larger numbers of students from certain leading Japanese universities results in large numbers of directors and presidents of companies being graduates from the same universities. In this sense, universities can create *gakubatsu*, academic cliques, at companies. But this is generally limited to a small number of leading universities such as the University of Tokyo and Keio University. The remaining approximately 600 universities in Japan are not generally associated with corporate *gakubatsu*.

East Japan Railways Co., the Industrial Bank of Japan, Ltd., Nippon Steel Corp., the Fuji Bank Ltd., Fanuc Ltd., the

ック、東京三菱銀行、日本たばこ産業、東京電力などの企業で、役員の中で東大出身者の占める比率は50%を超えています。

　慶応大出身役員の比率が高いのは三井倉庫、佐々木硝子、三越、千代田生命保険、三井不動産、鐘紡などの三井系企業で、比率はやはり50%を超えています。

　京都大学は関西系企業での役員比率は高いのですが、東大や慶応ほど特定企業に集中してはいません。一橋大学は役員や社長になる人は多いのですが、特定の企業への偏りはみられません。早稲田大学は一部マスコミでは学閥を形成していますが、一般企業では目立った閥はありません。

　企業ではありませんが、中央官庁の幹部職員は東大出身者が圧倒的多数を占め、「学閥」との批判を浴びています。また地方企業には地元大学出身者が大勢入社するので、役員の中で地元大学出身者の比率が高くなり、結果的に学閥を形成することもあります。

Bank of Tokyo Mitsubushi, Japan Tobacco Inc. and Tokyo Electric Power Co., Inc. are all renowned for containing Tokyo University cliques. More than 50 percent of directors at these companies were students at the University of Tokyo.

Companies that have a high ratio of directors who are former Keio University students include the Mitsui Group companies including Mitsui-Soko Co., Ltd., Sasaki Glass Co., Ltd., Mitsukoshi Ltd., the Chiyoda Mutual Life Insurance Co., Mitsui Fudosan Co., Ltd., and Kanebo, Ltd. Keio graduates make up more than half of the number of all the directors at these corporations.

Graduates from the University of Kyoto make up a high proportion of directors at companies in the Kansai region, surrounding Kyoto and Osaka, but they are not grouped at specific companies to the extent of either Tokyo or Keio graduates. Many former students from Hitotsubashi University are directors or presidents of companies but there is no trend of them joining certain predetermined organizations. Some graduates from Waseda University have formed cliques within the media but there are no obvious Waseda cliques in ordinary Japanese businesses.

Unlike industry, in central government University of Tokyo graduates hold an overwhelming number of executive positions, which has led to criticism. At regional companies large numbers of graduates from the region where a company is located are recruited and thus a very high proportion of directors are graduates from these local universities. This has also resulted in the formation of academic cliques.

・**64**

Question | 会社での男女の待遇は同じですか？

Answer | 日本の会社では長い間、女性は男性の補助的な仕事しか与えられず、採用や昇進、給与などの面で差別を受けてきました。社内の昇進試験を受けさせてもらえない、結婚後は退職を強制された、結婚しても退職しなかったら給料を下げられた、など差別の例は数限りなくありました。「女性は結婚退職が当然」と公言する大企業もあったほどです。

こうした差別待遇の解消を目指して1986年に男女雇用機会均等法が施行されました。背景には国連の「女子に対するあらゆる形態の差別の撤廃に関する条約」の批准問題もありました。施行後は企業は露骨な差別はしにくくなりましたが、実際にはあまり改善されたとはいえません。

日本の労働人口の約40％に当たる2700万人余りが女性ですが、女性管理職の比率は全産業で約10％、銀行はわずか2％程度です。役員になるともっと低く、97年に東洋経済新報社が上場企業など2413社を対象に調査したところ、全役員4万4925人のうち女性は82人、兼務

• 64

Q: Are men and women treated equally at Japanese companies?

A: For a long time women in Japanese companies were only given jobs assisting men in their work. Women were discriminated against when it came to recruitment, promotion and salaries. Women were not allowed to sit internal tests or evaluations for promotion. After getting married they were forced to leave the company and there are many recorded cases of discrimination including salary reductions for women who refused to resign following marriage. Some major companies even openly declared that female employees must quit their jobs after getting married.

In 1986 to put an end to this form of discrimination the Equal Employment Opportunities Law was enacted. The introduction of this legislation was also associated with problems surrounding Japan's ratification of the United Nations' Convention on the Elimination of All Forms of Discrimination against Women. Following this it has become difficult for companies to be overtly discriminatory against women but in reality there has been very little improvement.

About 40 percent of Japan's working population, some 27 million people, are women. However, the percentage of management positions held by women in all Japanese industry is just 10 percent and in banks it is a mere 2 percent. The number of women becoming directors is even lower. According to a survey conducted by the publisher Toyo Keizai Inc., of

を含めた延べ人数は84人、率にすると、なんと0.18%でした。

　差別が解消されない原因の一つは、均等法が募集・採用、配置・昇進についての男女の均等な取り扱いを雇用主の「努力義務」とするなど、不十分な内容だったためです。99年4月から男女の差別禁止を明確化した「改正均等法」が施行される予定で、今度こそ解消が期待されています。

・**65**

Question | 日本の社内教育の実態は？

Answer | 日本の企業は、自社の社風に合わせようと社員に対し、さまざまな研修や教育を施しています。
　手始めは入社時の研修です。電話の受け答えから名刺の渡し方、お辞儀の仕方、自己紹介の仕方など社会人としてのマナーをたたき込まれます。メーカーの場合など大学卒の幹部候補生でも、研修で数週間から数ヵ月間、工場勤務をさせられるケースもあります。

all 2,413 Japanese companies floated on the stock exchange amongst the 44,925 directors only 82 were women. If one includes women who hold more than one position at these companies the total rises to 84. As a percentage of the total number of directors this is a mere 0.18 percent.

One of the reasons that discrimination has not been reduced in Japan is that the Equal Employment Opportunities Law is insufficient as it only requires companies to officially "make efforts" towards equality when it comes to recruitment, appointments, posting and promotions. In April 1999, a revision of the law which will clearly prohibit discrimination between men and women is planned. Many people hope this will finally bring an end to sexual discrimination in Japan.

• 65

Q: What is the state of in-house training programs at Japanese corporations?

A: Japanese companies conduct various types of training and educational programs for their staff to bring them in line with company corporate culture.

This commences with training upon entering a company which is designed to knock new recruits' manners into shape by teaching them how to answer the telephone, how to hand out business cards, how to bow, and how to make personal introductions. Some manufacturers even make university graduates who are candidates for executive positions within their organizations, train on the factory floor for several weeks or months.

　さらに入社3年目や10年目、昇格とかいろ
いろな機会を捉えて研修を行う企業がありま
す。「地獄の特訓」と称して特別に厳しい訓練施設
に中堅幹部を2週間ほど送り込む会社もありま
す。これなどは知識取得とか、社員を鍛える
のが目的ではなく、厳しい訓練に耐えられな
いような社員を追い出すための口実づくりと
もいわれています。

　優雅なのは語学や経営知識取得のため、外
国の大学や大学院へ留学生として派遣される
場合です。大手企業や中央官庁は毎年、20代
の社員や職員の中から数人ないし10数人を選
び、1年か2年、欧米の有名大学、大学院に留
学させます。授業料はすべて会社や官庁持ち
で給料も出ます。送り出す方は社員、職員教
育の一環と位置付けています。

　しかし、最近は留学先で経営学修士号（M
BA）を取得した社員が、帰国後その資格を武
器に外資系企業に転職するケースも多く、社
命留学など社員への長期的な教育投資は企業
にとって割に合わなくなってきています。い
ずれ見直しの動きが出てくるかもしれません。

Furthermore, Japanese companies use many opportunities to provide additional training such as training schemes held 3 years and 10 years after initially joining a company, as well as special training before promotion to section head or department head. Some companies send middle management executives to special training facilities for up to two weeks for what is dubbed by many as "training hell". The aim of this type of training is not to improve staff skills or to help staff acquire new knowledge; it is said to be a pretext for driving out staff from the company who cannot endure the rigorous training.

But luxury training schemes do also exist. These generally consist of being sent overseas to university or graduate school for foreign language training or to acquire specialist business management skills. Major corporations and central government offices choose a few dozen people every year in their 20s to study abroad for 1 or 2 years at famous universities and graduate schools in the United States and Europe. All tuition fees are paid by the companies or the government and the employees also receive full salaries. The organizations who send staff overseas view this as part of general staff education and human resource development.

However, recently many people who have gone overseas to study for a Master of Business Administration (MBA) on their return to Japan use their new qualification as a weapon for getting new jobs at foreign companies. These long-term substantial investments that companies have been making in training their staff, by for example sending them overseas, are no longer paying off for corporate Japan and this will probably lead to a reappraisal of the existing system.

• 66

Question
Answer

日本企業はストックオプションを導入していますか?

ストックオプションというのは、企業が役員や社員に対しあらかじめ決めておいた価格で自社株を購入する権利を与え、企業の業績が向上、株価が上がれば権利を行使して株の売却益が得られる制度です。

この制度のおかげでアメリカの急成長企業の社員に億万長者が続出、それがアメリカ経済の活力の元にもなっていることに刺激され、日本でもベンチャー企業には95年11月、株式公開企業には97年6月から解禁されました。

97年末時点で早くも上場企業、店頭公開企業など80社近くが導入、検討中の企業は数百社にも達しています。

解禁されたばかりですから権利の付与対象者や行使期間などは企業によってバラバラです。トヨタ自動車、ニチメンは取締役だけを付与対象とするなど、大企業ほど対象を幹部に限定する傾向にあります。中堅企業の中には全社員を対象にしているところもあります。

ストックオプションは、使い方によっては役員や社員に対し長期目標達成のためのイン

• 66

Q: Are stock options being introduced in Japan?

A: Stock options are when a company allows directors and employees to purchase stocks in the company they work for at a set price. People can profit from these rights by selling the stocks at a profit, when the company's profits and share price rise.

Thanks to this system employees of rapidly expanding companies have become billionaires. This has been one of the factors behind increased economic activity in the United States. To stimulate similar activity in Japan the prohibition on stock options was lifted for venture businesses in Japan in November 1995, and for publicly traded companies in June 1997.

At the end of 1997, close to 80 floated companies in Japan and companies whose shares are traded on the over-the-counter market quickly introduced stock option schemes and several hundred other companies are considering doing so.

As stock options have only just been allowed, the types of people given stock options and the period of exercise differs widely from company to company. Toyota Motor Corp. and Nichimen Corp. have given options only to directors and many major corporations tend to limit them to senior executives. Some small and medium sized companies, however, have given stock options to all employees.

Depending how stock options are used they can become long-term incentives for directors and employees. But they

センティブ効果がありますが、一方で年功序列型賃金制度を破壊しかねません。企業は、こうしたメリットとデメリットを考えながら導入について模索している段階のようです。

　もっとも、いまのように株価が長期低空飛行を続けている状態では、権利を付与されてもそれを行使する機会がなかなかないかもしれませんが。

breakdown the traditional seniority based wage system. Companies are currently at the stage of trying to weigh up the merits and disadvantages of stock options. Japanese share prices have been constantly low for a long time and even if one is given such rights, currently there is hardly any chance of exercising them at a profit.

「サラリーマンの通勤事情」

「**睡**眠は電車とわが家で8時間」——第一生命保険会社が毎年募集しているサラリーマン川柳コンクールの入賞作品の一つです。疲れ気味のサラリーマンが電車の座席で熟睡する姿が目に浮かぶようです。

　ただ、東京の通勤電車で座席に座れるのは超ラッキーな人か、通勤時間が2時間を超えるような超長距離通勤者で、始発電車に乗れる人に限られます。通勤1時間から1時間半の「中距離通勤者」は、座席で眠り込む人を横目に満員電車で立ちっぱなしの毎日です。

　電車の混み方も半端じゃなく、ホームの駅員が乗客の背中を押して車内に押し込むほどで、ほとんど家畜並み、いやそれ以下の扱いです。だから会社に着いた後はしばらく休まないと仕事になりません。日本のサラリーマンは、1日に消費するエネルギーの半分近くを朝夕の通勤に費やしているのが実感です。

　ちなみに東京で一番混むといわれる新宿駅の1日の乗降客は300万人を超えており、池袋駅や渋谷駅も200万人から300万人の乗降客がいます。

　こうした通勤地獄に耐えられず、会社の近くにワンルームマンションを借り、平日はそこから通勤、週末だけ家族の住む郊外の自宅に帰る企業戦士もいます。通勤地獄は経済全体からみると壮大な無駄ですが、人口に比べ交通手段が貧弱な東京を中心とする首都圏では、解消のめどは全く立っていません。

The *salaryman's* commute

The phrase, "I sleep a total of 8 hours a day on the train and at home" won a prize at the Dai-ichi Mutual Life Insurance Co., Ltd.'s annual *salaryman senryu*, seventeen-syllable satirical poetry, competition which brings to mind the image of a *salaryman* sound asleep on a train seat.

But the reality is one has to be incredibly lucky to get a seat on a train in Tokyo. This luxury is normally limited to people with really long commutes of more than two hours who get on at the first stop. Everyday, commuters with journeys of one or one and a half hours stand in packed trains looking out of the corner of their eyes at the lucky few seated and sound asleep.

It is not just people getting crushed on trains. On the platforms the railway staff shove people in the back, herding them into trains like cattle, probably in a manner even worse than cattle. So it is essential to rest for awhile after arriving at the office. Japanese *salaryman* feel as if half of the energy they consume everyday is expended during the morning and evening rush hours.

Shinjuku Station in Tokyo is said to be the most crowded station in Japan. 3 million passengers get off at Shinjuku Station everyday. At Ikebukuro Station and Shibuya Station, also in Tokyo, between 2 and 3 million people get off or change trains everyday.

This commuting hell becomes unbearable and some "corporate warriors" rent one room apartments near their companies from which they commute during the week, only returning to their family homes in the suburbs at the weekends. From the economy's point of view this commuting hell is an utter waste. Compared with the population the transportation facilities are totally inadequate in Tokyo, a huge central metropolis, where the prospects of resolving the problem seem almost nonexistent.

日本のサラリーマン
PART 2

Working in Corporate Japan: The *Salaryman*
PART 2

・67

Question　日本の接待の実態は？

Answer　接待の主流はお酒とゴルフです。銀座には何千軒ものクラブやバーがあり、ホステスさんが相手をしてくれますが、ほとんどが企業の接待用なので値段はべらぼうです。

　日本ではビジネス客を自宅に招く習慣はありません。サラリーマンの自宅は遠い郊外にあり、しかも狭くて人を招くなどとてもできないからです。その代わりクラブや料亭などで接待するのです。

　ゴルフもレクレーションやスポーツというより、接待の手段として普及してきました。クラブハウスなどは異常に豪華で、1日のプレー代も3万円から5万円もします。地価が高いのも一因ですが、プレー代は会社が払うという悪しき習慣が定着したのが原因です。最近は海外での接待も増えています。

　国税庁の調査によると、企業がこうした接待に使う交際費は96年1年間で約5兆4000億円に達しています。

　民間企業同士が接待するのは違法ではありませんが、公務員を接待すると汚職になります。98年には銀行や証券会社から接待を受け

• 67

Q: What is the truth about Japanese corporate entertainment, *settai*?

A: *Settai*, corporate entertainment in Japan, usually consists of drinking or playing golf. In Ginza there are thousands of bars and clubs where hostesses entertain customers. As the majority of these establishments are used for corporate entertainment they have absurdly high prices.

In Japan the convention of inviting clients to one's home does not exist. *Salarymen* generally live far out in the suburbs in small homes which makes entertaining at home impossible. Instead, customers are entertained at clubs and restaurants.

Golf spread in Japan more as a form of corporate entertainment than as a recreational activity or sport. Club houses on golf courses are extremely luxurious and one day's play can cost between 30,000 and 50,000 yen. One reason for this is the high cost of land in Japan. However, the real reason is probably due to the bad, but now well established habit, of companies picking up the bill for a game of golf. Recently entertaining Japanese clients overseas has increased.

According to a survey by the National Tax Administration Agency, the amount spent for corporate entertainment reached 5 trillion 400 billion yen in 1996.

It is not illegal for private companies to entertain staff at other companies but the entertainment of public servants can cause corruption. In 1998, a string of executives from

た大蔵省や日銀の幹部が相次いで逮捕されました。特定の公務員に対する接待があまりに目立ったため、「一罰百戒」の意味を込めて処分されたのです。

事件後、政府は、接待自粛のお触れを出しましたが、自粛が長く続くとは思えません。ほとぼりが冷めるとまたぞろ復活するでしょう。これまでもその繰り返しでした。接待の歴史は1000年前の平安時代までさかのぼるという説もあり、この習慣は一朝一夕にはなくなりそうもありません。

• **68**

Question | **社内いじめの実態は？**

Answer | 社内いじめにはリストラ対象の中高年や女性社員を対象にした「組織ぐるみのいじめ」と、「個人的ないじめ」の2種類があります。不況で最近増えているのは組織ぐるみのいじめです。

組織ぐるみのいじめの狙いははっきりしています。いじめや嫌がらせに音を上げて、本人が退職せざるを得なくさせるが最大の狙いです。絶対に達成できない営業のノルマを課したり、逆に仕事を一切与えず窓際に追いやり、「社内村八分」にしたり、毎日毎日、上司

the Ministry of Finance and the Bank of Japan who received lavish entertainment from banks and security companies were arrested. The entertainment of certain bureaucrats became so obvious that it was dealt with by these arrests which are designed to act as a deterrent for other bureaucrats.

Afterwards the government imposed a moratorium on entertainment but this moratorium is unlikely to last long. Once the current furor has blown over it will no doubt start again. This is what has happened in the past. Japanese style corporate entertainment is said to have started 1,000 years ago back in the Heian Period (794–1192) and it seems very unlikely to disappear overnight.

• 68

Q: Does bullying occur within Japanese companies?

A: There are two main types of bullying at Japanese companies "institutionalized bullying" of old and middle-aged employees or female workers who are targeted during corporate restructuring or down-sizing and "individual bullying." The recent recession in Japan has led to an increase in the former.

The aim of institutionalized bullying is clearly to make people react to the bullying and harassment and force them to resign. Bullying takes many forms including handing out impossible business assignments, or the opposite, taking away work and driving staff to sit by the window in a form of ostracism, being criticized day after day by the boss about

が仕事のことで責めたり、会社の損を補てんするよう迫ったりとやり方はいろいろです。

　いじめの対象者が最終的に辞めてくれればいいので、本人が辞表を提出すると上司は急に優しくなったりします。

　個人的ないじめは▽お茶の時間にお菓子やお茶を配らず、のけ者にする　▽昼食に誘わない　▽必要な書類を渡さない　▽悪口を言いふらす　▽先輩の高卒ＯＬが後輩の大卒ＯＬをつかまえてみんなの前で、「大卒なのにこんな書類も書けないの」となじる、といったケースなどです。「女の敵は女」で、女性による女性へのいじめも結構あります。

　同じ職場に正社員だけでなく契約社員や派遣社員、パート、アルバイトなどさまざまな立場の人が混在し、その中で一種の階級社会が形成され、会社内の「強者」と「弱者」が生まれていることも個人的ないじめの背景にあります。

one's work; or being pushed into "compensating" the company for its troubles.

The ultimate aim is to get those targeted for bullying to resign, so once a resignation letter has been handed in managers suddenly become kind and considerate.

There are many cases of individual bullying, being treated like an outcast, not being served tea and cakes at tea time, not being invited out for lunch, having essential business documents withheld, constant verbal abuse. A classic example is of a secretary (often referred to as office ladies or OLs in Japan) who has been educated up to high school level telling off a more junior university educated colleague in front of all the members of the office saying, "Even though you've been to university you can't write a simple document." It is often said that "a women's worst enemy is another woman" and bullying of women by other women in Japanese companies is quite common.

Japanese offices often contain a mix of people with various positions including permanent staff, contract workers, temporary workers from agencies, and part-timers, forming a type of employment class system, which has created a corporate environment that contains both the strong and the weak.

• 69

Question　日本ではＯＬの仕事は本当にお茶くみですか？

Answer　以前はＯＬの重要な仕事の一つはお茶くみとコピー取りでした。ある会社のある部署が社内の会議に女性を出席させるはずだったのが、予定変更で代わりに男性を出そうとしたら、「男じゃお茶くみができないから来る必要がない」と断られたというような話もありました。

　　ＯＬにお茶くみやコピー取りをやらせるのは、女性社員を一人前に扱わず、男性社員の補助業務をさせるという方針からきています。補助業務にはお茶くみやコピー取りだけでなく、電話番や個人的な買い物、男性社員の出張精算などが含まれることもありました。家庭で妻が夫の世話をするように、会社では女性社員が男性社員の世話をみるという発想です。

　　しかし、こうした男性優位の慣習も過去のものになりつつあります。いまは女性だけにお茶を入れさせるような差別はできませんし、企業もお茶くみのために女性社員を雇う余裕はありません。女性も男性も仕事の上では区別せず、お茶くみやコピー取りも自分でする会社が多くなりました。来客へのお茶出しも

• 69

Q: **In Japan are office ladies really employed to make tea?**

A: One of the most important jobs for office ladies (OLs) used to be making tea and taking photocopies. This is highlighted by a classic story that at one Japanese company a women was supposed to attend an internal company meeting but plans changed and a man was sent in her place. However, he was told not to bother coming to the meeting as men cannot make tea.

The idea that OLs should make tea and take photocopies comes from not treating female employees as equals and the principle that they are there to assist men in their business activities. Providing assistance is not just limited to making tea and taking photocopies. It also involves answering the telephone, buying things for male members of staff and calculating expense claims for male colleagues. The concept behind this is that female employees should look after their male colleagues in the office in the same way as a wife looks after her husband at home.

However, this system of male superiority is quickly becoming a thing of the past. Now discrimination such as requiring female employees to make tea (for male members of staff) is not allowed and companies no longer have the flexibility to employ women just for making tea. The number of Japanese companies that do not discriminate between men and women and require staff to make their own cups of

若手の男女社員が交代でやるところもあります。

　ただ、いまもなお女性にお茶くみを「強制」している企業もあります。特に古い伝統のある大企業や役所などにはそういう体質が残っているようです。ある調査によると、OLの約6割は「お茶くみはいやだ」と答えているのですが…。

• 70

Question　社内不倫と玉の輿、日本の会社ではよくあることですか？

Answer　男と女が一緒に仕事をしているうちに自然に仲良くなるのは、どこの国、どこの会社でも起きることでしょう。未婚同士ならば結婚にゴールインしてハッピーエンドですが、どちらかが既婚者の場合は不倫になります。

　日本の会社は、一般的にお金と異性問題にはうるさいです。少額でも会社のお金に手をつけたらクビですし、経費の水増し請求が分かっても人事評価はガタ落ちです。社内不倫も発覚したら男性が既婚者の場合、男性の出世の見込みはほとんどなくなり、場合によっては退職を余儀なくされます。女性も居心地が悪くなり、辞めざるを得なくなるケースが多いようです。

tea and take their own photocopies is on the increase. Young male and female employees often now take turns in serving tea to visiting customers.

Even today there are still companies that make it compulsory for women to make tea. This characteristic remains prevalent especially in major traditional companies and government offices. According to one survey 60 percent of women say that they hate serving tea at their offices but...

• 70

Q: Is adultery and *tama-no-koshi*, marrying money, common within Japanese companies?

A: It is only natural that men and women who work in close proximity become friends. This happens in companies and countries throughout the world. In Japan it is often the ultimate goal for single men and woman to marry colleagues from work and it is considered a happy end if they achieve this. But close relationships between married people at work often lead to adultery.

Japanese companies are in general very strict about money, and sexual relationships with other members of staff. Employees will be fired for stealing even small amounts of money and reputations can be ruined if someone is discovered making exaggerated expense claims. If a married man is discovered having an affair with someone in the company it is extremely unlikely he will ever be promoted and sometimes he will be forced to resign. The position of women implicated in extra-marital affairs becomes very difficult

　日本の会社の「不倫度」が、外国に比べて高いか低いかはわかりませんが、「失楽園」という不倫を題材にした小説がベストセラーになり、映画もヒットしたことを考えると、ビジネスマンとOLには不倫への願望があると思われます。

　一方、OLが社内や社外の名門もしくは資産家の御曹司と結婚したりすると、周囲はやっかみ半分に、女性のことを「玉の輿に乗る」と評します。

「輿」は平安、鎌倉時代に貴族が利用した乗り物で、「玉」は立派なという意味。つまり「低い身分に生まれたけれど、立派な輿に乗るような高い身分に上ることができた」という喩えです。現代の日本には身分制度はないので「お金持ちと結婚できた」という意味合いになります。玉の輿に乗れるかどうかは、本人の努力（？）と2人の相性にかかっています。

　女性が有力者や資産家のお嬢様で、男性がフツーの家庭出身の場合は「逆・玉の輿」、略して「逆玉」と言います。

and in most cases they are forced to resign.

It is not known whether the infidelity rate at Japanese companies is higher than that of companies overseas, but when one considers the success of the best selling novel "Shitsurakuen", paradise lost, about an affair between young workers and the success of the film based on the book, it raises the question whether Japanese businessmen and office ladies yearn for similar experiences.

On the other hand, if an office lady marries a man who comes from a distinguished or wealthy Japanese family people will remark that she is set to ride a *tama-no-koshi*.

A *koshi* was a carriage used by aristocrats in the Heian (794–1192) and Kamakura periods (1192–1333) and *tama* means magnificent. This metaphor literally means that despite being born as a person of low station you have been lifted up to a high rank onto a magnificent carriage. Japan no longer has a class system and the expression is now used to mean marrying into wealth. Whether one gets the possibility of riding a *tama-no-koshi*, magnificent carriage, depends on an individual's efforts and a couple's compatibility.

If a capable girl from a rich family marries a man from an ordinary simple background this is described as *gyaku tama-no-koshi* or *gyaku-tama* for short, a reverse magnificent carriage.

・71

Question 天下り、天上がりというのは何のことですか？

Answer 神々が住むといわれる「天」から人間が住む「下界」へおりることを日本では「天下り」と言います。それが転じて役所を退職した高級官僚が、関連の団体や民間会社に有利な条件で再就職することを「天下り」というようになりました。

　日本では昔から役人が強い権限を持っています。800年ぐらい前の鎌倉時代に税金などを取り立てる「地頭」という役人がいて「泣く子と地頭には勝てぬ」という諺があったほどです。

　天下りを受け入れる企業が役人に期待するのは、役所とのパイプ役です。許認可などで役所と交渉する場合、官僚OBを抱えていれば手続きなどがスムーズに運ぶ可能性があります。運輸や金融など許認可の多い企業ほど役人を受け入れるはそのためです。

　世論の批判を浴びて政府は天下りを規制しようとしていますが、効果はなく、今も毎年多くの役人が企業などに天下っています。天下りの数は省庁によって違いますが、大蔵省の場合、97年8月時点で金融・証券界だけでも514人が天下っています。

　「天上がり」は、企業の社員が官庁に2、3年

• 71

Q: What is *ama-kudari* and *ama-agari*?

A: The fall or descent from heaven, where gods are said to live, to earth where humans live is what is literally meant by *ama-kudari* in Japanese. But the meaning has been changed and *ama-kudari* now refers to when high-ranking bureaucrats retire and join related organizations or private companies under advantageous conditions.

Historically Japanese bureaucrats have been very powerful. About 800 years ago in the Kamakura period (1192–1333) there were officials called *jito*, lords of the manor, who collected taxes. They were so strong willed it was said that "you cannot win against a crying child or a *jito*."

Companies that employ officials through *ama-kudari* expect them to act as communication pipes to the ministries they came from. Using an "old-boy" from the ministry during license applications and other negotiations helps smooth the application process. Companies that require many transport and finance licenses take on board officials for this purpose.

Critical public opinion has led to moves to regulate *ama-kudari* but they have been ineffectual and even now every year many officials join companies through *ama-kudari*. The number of people getting jobs through *ama-kudari* differs at each ministry. But in August 1997 there were 514 people working at financial firms alone who had got their jobs through *ama-kudari* from the Ministry of Finance.

Ama-agari is when company employees join ministries

間出向することです。給料は企業持ちで役所
の仕事を手伝います。企業側は「研修」と称
していますが、狙いは役所とのパイプ作り。
優秀な幹部候補生が選ばれますから役所にと
っても貴重な戦力になり、官民の間に持ちつ
持たれつの関係が成立します。天上がりが官
民癒着、汚職の温床になっているとの批判の
声も根強くあります。

・72

Question｜**日本の会社ではセクハラは問題になっ
ていますか？**

Answer｜これまではあまり問題にはなっていませんで
したが、三菱自動車工業アメリカ工場で起き
たセクハラ事件をきっかけに、クローズアッ
プされるようになりました。

　日本でこれまでセクハラが表面化しなかっ
たのは、女性が泣き寝入りしていたためと思
われます。日本の社会、特に企業や役所は男
性中心で、女性は男性と同等には扱われてい
ませんでした。女性が結婚したら退職を強制
する会社がつい最近まであったくらいです。

　日本の企業や役所には、仕事中に女性社員
の体に触ったり、新婚の女性社員に「こども
はまだ？　作り方を教えてあげようか」など
の暴言を吐く中年社員がゴマンといました。

on temporary loan for 2 or 3 years. Their salaries are paid by their companies but they assist the ministries with their work. Companies call this "training" and aim to build communication pipes with the ministries. Fast track executives are chosen and it becomes an important tactic for the ministries in building strong relations with the private sector. *Ama-agari* people and bureaucrats stick together and are strongly criticized for being a hotbed of corruption.

• 72

Q: Is sexual harassment a problem at Japanese companies?

A: Up until recently sexual harassment has not been an issue at Japanese companies but the case of widespread sexual harassment at a Mitsubishi Motors Corp.'s factory in the United States has highlighted the issue.

In Japan until now sexual harassment has not come to the surface, probably because women have put up with it. Japanese society in general and particularly Japanese companies and government offices are male oriented and women have not been treated equally. Until recently most Japanese companies ordered women to resign after they got married and companies like these still probably exist today.

In Japanese companies and government offices during working hours lots of middle-aged male employees used to fondle female employees and make abusive remarks to newly-weds, for example, saying, "No children yet? Shall I show you how it's done?"

　社員旅行の宴会で女性社員に酒のお酌を強制するのは良くあること、女性社員の前で裸踊りをする男性社員もいます。こうしたセクハラ行為が予想されるため、多くの女性社員は社員旅行を嫌がっています。

　中にはセクハラ行為も軽く受け流す太っ腹の女性社員もいますが、大部分の女性は男性中心社会の悪習にじっとがまんしてきたと思います。

　98年3月、日本政府の人事部に当たる人事院は、国家公務員を対象にした初のセクハラ実態調査の結果を発表しました。それによると、「職場内外で性的関係を強要されたことがある」と答えた女性は、6人に1人にあたる17%にも上ることが明らかになりました。こうした実態を踏まえて人事院はセクハラ防止策をまとめる予定で、企業もようやくセクハラ防止に動き出しています。

・73

Question　**社宅や保養所などサラリーマンの給料以外の余禄は？**

Answer　一般的な余禄としてはまず住宅関係が挙げられます。社宅や独身寮、単身赴任者用の寮、家賃補助、住宅取得のための低利融資などです。

During banquets on company trips female employees were often forced to serve *sake* for male employees and sometimes male colleagues even danced naked in front of their female colleagues. Many women hate company trips because they know how they can end up.

Some thick skinned Japanese female employees brush aside this type of sexual harassment but the vast majority of Japanese women have until now had to endure patiently this abusive male oriented behavior.

In March 1998, the National Personnel Authority, the personnel department for the Japanese government, published the results of the first ever survey on sexual harassment amongst government officials. The survey showed that 1 in 6 women (17 percent) had been pressured sexually in and outside the workplace. The National Personnel Authority is planning an anti-sexual harassment policy to try to control the situation. Japanese companies have also finally started making moves to put an end to sexual harassment within their organizations.

• 73

Q: What fringe benefits do *salarymen* get in addition to their salaries?

A: The most common type of fringe benefits in Japan are related to accommodation. Various types of benefits exist such as *shataku* (company provided accommodation), company dormitories for unmarried staff, special accommodation and dormitories for staff on *tanshin-funin* (living separately from

　各種グラウンドやテニスコート、プールを持つ企業は多く、会社帰りに社員が汗を流せるよう民間のスポーツクラブと契約している会社もあります。たいていの大企業は全国の観光地に保養所を持っています。

　大企業の本社や工場には社員食堂があり、食事代はタダという会社さえあります。ほとんどの企業は通勤費を支給しますが、欧米企業のように「カンパニーカー」を支給することはありません。

　メーカーの場合、社員は自社製品を割引価格で買えたり、運輸関係企業では、自社の鉄道や航空便を無料か、格安料金で利用できます。銀行より高い金利で社員からお金を預かる社内預金制度を持つ企業もあります。

　勤続20年や30年の節目に社員に慰労金を支給したり、社員が結婚した場合の祝い金や、家族が死亡した場合に香典を出すのも一般的です。

　こうした給与以外の余禄は大企業ほど充実しています。給与だけでなく、余禄面でも大企業と中小企業は格差があるのが現状です。

　ただ、最近は保養所などを閉鎖して福利厚生サービスの代行会社と契約したり、社宅を

their families due to a posting), rental assistance, and low interest rate loans for acquiring property.

Many companies own different types of sports facilities including tennis courts and swimming pools. Other companies sign agreements with private sports clubs and gyms so their staff can work out on the way home. Most major Japanese corporations own and run facilities and health centers, which their staff can use, at tourist resorts across Japan.

At the headquarters and factories of major Japanese companies there are almost always staff canteens which serve meals; in somes cases for free. The majority of companies in Japan subsidize commuting travel costs but unlike the United States and Europe, Japanese companies do not pay for company cars.

Manufacturers allow their staff to purchase company products at a discount and transport companies allow staff to travel free or at significant discounts on their trains or airplanes. Some companies run saving schemes for their staff which pay higher interest rates than banks. It is also standard practice for Japanese companies to pay their staff special gratuities for all their hard work after 20 years and 30 years of service, to give staff gifts of money to congratulate them on getting married and to pay condolence money when a member of an employee's family dies.

These types of benefits paid in addition to the monthly salaries are especially well established at large corporations. The difference between working for large, medium and small sized corporations is reflected not just in salary size but in the generosity of these benefits.

However, recently the number of companies closing their privately run health centers and signing contracts with

売却したりする企業も増えています。「休みの日まで会社の人と顔を合わせたくない」という社員の意識変化に加え、大手企業では社員一人当たり年間100万円を超えるといわれる福利厚生費が、企業にとって負担になってきているという事情もあります。

・74

Question 日本ではなぜ単身赴任が多いのですか？

Answer 日本では約30万人のサラリーマンが単身赴任をしているといわれますが、さまざまな理由から、この習慣は当分なくなりそうもありません。

　一つは頻繁な人事異動にあります。大手企業の場合、同じポストにいる期間は2、3年で、春に「定期異動」という形で全社的な人事異動を行う会社が多く、社員は異動を拒否することはできません。

　転勤の場合、家族そろって赴任するとなると、子供の教育や病人、配偶者の仕事などの問題を解決しなければなりません。

　小、中学校は全国どこでも子供を受け入れてくれますが、高校は義務教育ではありませ

companies that run health and welfare services, or selling the company staff residences is increasing. Employee sentiment has also changed. Company employees no longer want to see the faces of their colleagues on their days off and major Japanese corporations are now loaded down with welfare expenses which have reached more than 1 million yen per employee every year.

• 74

Q: Is *tanshin-funin*, taking a post in another city or country alone leaving one's family behind, common in Japan?

A: 300,000 *salarymen* are thought to live alone away from their families, in what is known as *tanshin-funin*. There are many reasons for this and at present it seems unlikely that this practice will disappear.

One reason is the frequency of staff rotations in Japan. In major Japanese corporations people hold the same post for only 2 or 3 years and every spring at a fixed time many Japanese companies conduct company wide staff rotations. Employees cannot refuse requests for them to move to new positions or sections.

Transfers to other parts of the country present difficulties for employees as taking the whole family creates a host of problems associated with children's education, looking after elderly or infirm relatives and spouses' jobs.

Primary schools and junior high schools throughout the country will always take in new students. But high school edu-

んので、途中編入は認められず、転校はほとんど不可能です。

　配偶者が仕事を持っていても会社はそれを考慮しませんので、配偶者は仕事を辞めるか、別居かの選択を迫られます。病気の家族や老人がいる場合も引っ越しは非常に難しくなります。

　結局、家族そろって赴任できるのは子供が小さく、配偶者が仕事を持っていない場合などに限られ、40代や50代のサラリーマンの多くは単身赴任を強いられているのが現状です。

　それでも国内なら月に1回か2回は家族のもとに帰れますが、海外勤務の場合はそうもいかず、長期の単身赴任を強いられた結果、夫婦間が疎遠になったり、子供が非行に走ったりと、さまざま問題も起きています。

・75

Question　**日本の会社ではパソコンが出来ないと落ちこぼれますか？**

Answer　文章作成やメールの送受信などパソコンの初歩的な操作ぐらいはできないと、たいていの会社では業務に支障が出ますので、落ちこぼれる可能性が十分にあります。会社によっては、出社した社員の最初の仕事は、まず社内各部署からのメールを読むというところもありますから。

　日本ＩＢＭは、約2万1000人の社員全員にパ

cation is not part of the Japanese compulsory education system and these schools thus will not take in new students once a term has started. Changing schools is practically impossible.

A spouse's job will not be taken into consideration by the company, which leaves two options—quitting the job or living apart. If sick or aged members of the family need to be looked after, moving becomes extremely difficult.

Subsequently, taking the whole family is limited to when children are young and when a spouse does not have a job. The reality is that many *salarymen* in their 40s and 50s end up doing *tanshin-funin* and living alone.

If the transfer is within Japan, it is usual to visit one's family once or twice a month but in the case of an overseas posting this is impossible. Couples can spend a long time apart, which can lead to all sorts of difficulties. Couples can drift apart and children can even end up becoming delinquents.

• 75

Q: What happens to people in Japanese companies who cannot use computers?

A: If you cannot use a computer to write simple documents or to send and receive e-mail it is almost impossible to do any work. This can lead to staff falling behind on the promotion ladder and even becoming a corporate drop-out. At many Japanese companies the day begins by checking e-mail from other sections within the company.

IBM Japan Ltd. provides computers for all its 21,000

ソコンを支給、給料の明細などもメールで送っています。メールが読めないと自分の給料の内容すらわからないことになります。日本ＩＢＭはパソコンメーカーなので先進的なところもありますが、一般企業も社員全員にパソコンを支給する傾向にあり、稟議書や報告書などさまざまな社内文書は次第にメール化してきています。

　派遣社員の場合、パソコンを使えることが雇用の条件になっているケースが多く、一般社員もだんだん義務づけられるようになっています。

　パソコン支給に当たり会社は研修を行いますので、心配はないのですが、機械に弱い人はなかなか使いこなせず、苦労しているようです。社長をはじめ役員も例外ではなく、パソコンと格闘している中高年社員や役員は大勢おり、中高年専用のパソコン講座は大繁盛です。

　どうしてもマスターできない社員もいますが、そういう人は、特殊能力や技術を持っていない限り閑職に追いやられるか、リストラの対象になりかねません。

members of staff and even sends salary statements to its staff by e-mail. Not being able to read e-mail means not knowing how much you are getting paid each month. IBM Japan is a personal computer manufacturer and is more advanced than most Japanese companies in this respect. But there is not such a great difference between it and other companies in Japan. More and more companies in Japan are providing their staff with computers. Reports, company memoranda, and many other internal company documents are gradually being sent out in electronic form by e-mail.

Being able to use a personal computer is one of the employment prerequisites for temporary workers from agencies and it is rapidly becoming compulsory for regular employees to use computers.

When companies provide their staff with personal computers they run training courses so there is no real worry about learning how to operate them. But some people are not good with machines no matter how hard they try and they can end up suffering terribly. Many directors and middle-aged managers of Japanese companies are also currently grappling with computers. Special computer training courses for middle-aged people are very successful.

For people who are unable to master these machines only those who are held in high regard or have specialist knowledge or skills will avoid being shunted into unimportant positions within the company or losing their jobs altogether.

「カイシャの用語」

日本の会社には独特の用語があります。よく使われる用語を紹介すると…。

　お局様　平安時代の宮中の女官から転じて、ベテランOLを指します。小うるさく、若いOLからは煙たがられる存在です。

　腰掛け　希望が実現するまでの仮の職業、地位のこと。女性が、結婚までの短期間、会社に勤めることを指す言葉としてよく使います。

　総合職と一般職　1986年の男女雇用機会均等法の施行に伴い、男女別採用の代わりに、多くの企業が社員を総合職と一般職に分ける制度を導入しました。総合職は幹部候補生で、大卒男子はほとんど自動的に総合職になりますが、女性はほとんどが補助的な業務に従事する一般職に属します。

　根回し　ある事を提案したり実行する場合、事前に関係者に説明して話をつけておくこと。日本では組織内で何か実行する場合、いくら良いプランでも会議などで突然提案するとほとんどの場合、却下されるだけです。提案を認めてもらうには根回しが必要です。

　窓際族　会社で主流から外れ、窓際の閑職ポストに追いやられた社員を指しますが、最近の日本企業は、窓際族を抱える余裕もなくなり、かつての窓際族は肩たたきの対象になって会社から追い出されています。

Corporate nomenclature

Corporate Japan has its own special nomenclature. Here we introduce some of the most commonly used words.

Otsubone-sama, the traditional name for experienced ladies-in-waiting at the imperial court, during the Heian Period (1192–1333) has now been transformed into a word to describe long serving office ladies (OLs) who nag and annoy younger colleagues at the office.

Koshikake refers to the position of holding a provisional job until one's desired job is secured. It is also often used to refer to women who work for short periods in companies before getting married.

Sogo-shoku and *ippan-shoku*. In 1986, following the enactment of the Equal Opportunity Employment Law many companies introduced systems separating *sogo-shoku* and *ippan-shoku*, comprehensive work and ordinary work. Individuals who do *sogo-shoku* are potential candidates for executive positions. Almost all male university graduates automatically become *sogo-shoku* but the majority of women who are employed to work as assistants are *ippan-shoku*.

Nemawashi is when managers explain and discuss new work proposals with those involved before the plan is officially proposed. In Japan, within organizations, when something needs to be implemented no matter how good the plan is it will almost always be rejected if it is suddenly proposed during a meeting. To get a proposal accepted in Japan *nemawashi* is essential.

Madogiwa-zoku, literally "the tribe by the window," is when employees fall out of the mainstream within their companies become superfluous and are pushed into unimportant positions, and are given desks out of the way by the window. Recently, however, Japanese companies no longer have the resources to keep these so-called *madogiwa-zoku* employees on their payrolls. They now become the target of *katatataki*, tap on the shoulder, and are forced to resign and leave.

日本の会社に就職

Recruitment and
Employment in Japan

・**76**

Question | **就職協定って何ですか？**

Answer | 大学と企業が学生の就職活動について結ぶ取り決めのことです。毎年大学卒業者のうち40万人程度が就職しますが、石油ショック前の好景気のころ、企業はできるだけ早く優秀な学生を確保しようと採用活動を早め、1973年3月卒業予定者の採用活動は、学生がまだ4年生にもならない72年2月にはほとんど終わってしまいました。

　米商人が、稲が実る前に田んぼごと稲を買ったことにちなんで「青田買い」といわれ、このままエスカレートすれば、いずれは「大学入学と同時に採用内定」との冗談も出たほどです。

　しかし企業や大学関係者の間で「これはいかにもやりすぎ」との反省が生まれました。そして企業と大学が話し合い、釣りや狩猟の解禁みたいに学生の会社訪問と内定に解禁日を設定したわけです。
　しかし、協定ができても景気が良い時は、早めに学生を確保しようと抜け駆けする企業が後を絶たず、その後、協定はあまり守られ

• 76

Q: What is the recruitment pact?

A: The recruitment pact, *shushoku kyotei*, is an agreement between companies and universities about the hiring of students. Every year 400,000 students graduating from university are recruited by companies. But during the economic boom before the so-called oil shock, Japanese companies tried to recruit the brightest students as quickly as possible. This resulted in a situation where the majority of students planning to graduate from university in March 1973 had found jobs by February 1972, before they were even in their fourth and final year at university.

When Japanese rice merchants buy rice before it is ripe or harvested from the rice paddies it is called *aota-gai*, buying green rice from the fields. This expression is also used to describe Japanese companies recruiting young students. People began to worry that it would escalate further, leading to jokes that students might end up receiving unofficial job offers as soon as they entered university.

However, companies and universities thought this would be a deplorable situation. They started a dialogue and decided on restrictions similar to those for hunting and fishing, which limited interviews and *naitei*, unofficial job offers, to a certain season.

Nevertheless, during economic booms, companies constantly tried to get the edge on their competitors and recruit the best students, despite the existence of the pact. The pact

ないで有形無実となりました。このため日経連の根本二郎会長は96年末、97年度から会社訪問の解禁日を繰り上げると発表、事実上、就職協定は廃止されました。

今は会社の説明会や、学生の会社訪問の時期などは原則自由です。99年3月卒業予定者の場合、採用説明会は98年の4月か5月、正式内定の前の「内々定」を決めるピークは5月か6月ごろでした。

しかし、内定時期を早めると、その後の就職活動の結果、最初に決まった企業の内定を辞退する学生が増えるなど「歩留まり率」が悪化します。内定者が他の企業に逃げないように確保しておくことも人事担当者の重要な仕事になっています。

• 77

Question 「氷河期」「超・氷河期」とはいつの時代のことですか？

Answer バブル経済崩壊直後の94年の就職戦線はことのほか厳しく、身も凍り付くような「氷河期」と呼ばれました。企業は採用数を大幅に抑制、就職できずに大学で留年する「就職浪人」も大勢出ました。

翌95年はさらに厳しく「超・氷河期」と命名され、このままでは日本全体が氷河期に突

was rarely kept to, making it immaterial. This led to the lifting of the recruitment embargo for 1997 at the end of 1996 by Jiro Nemoto, the Chairman of the Federation of Employers Association, thereby abolishing the recruitment pact.

Now companies and students are in principle free to decide when to hold recruitment seminars and visit companies. Recruitment seminars were held in April and May 1998 for students planning to graduate from university in March 1999. The majority of "informal" job offers were made in May or June.

As companies make offers so early on, the number of students who reject these first informal offers for subsequent better ones is increasing, leading to a deteriorating acceptance rate. Making sure potential recruits who have been given job offers do not run off to other companies, is now becoming an important job for personnel managers in Japan.

• 77

Q: When was the ice age and the super ice age?

A: In 1994, after the collapse of Japan's economic bubble it was an extremely tough time for those on the front line looking for jobs. Opportunities were so scarce it was nicknamed the ice age. Companies dramatically cut their annual intake of new staff forcing many final year university students to remain at university for another year to prepare for the next annual job hunting round. They became known as *shushoku-ronin*, literally meaning "employment masterless samurais."

The next year, 1995, was even worse and dubbed the super ice age. The whole of Japan was thought to be about to

入するかとも思われました。幸い96年には状況はやや回復、「薄日がさした」「雪解け近し」と表現されました。

「就職協定廃止元年」となった翌97年は、企業の採用活動も早まるなど状況はさらに持ち直し、ようやく氷河期から抜け出しました。しかし、それも束の間、景気の後退で98年は再び行く手に暗雲が垂れ込み始めました。

暗雲が垂れ込めても一流大学の男子学生はまだ気楽。深刻なのは女子学生です。一流大学を卒業しても女性の就職は依然として厳しい環境にあります。どの企業も管理部門の効率化を図るため、事務職の採用を減らしています。男女雇用機会均等法という法律はありますが、男性とまったく同じ働きを求められる職種では、実際の就職の際は女性の方が不利になるからです。

不景気が続くと女性の就職戦線は再び氷河期に突入しそうです。次の氷河期に備えて女性の間では医師、弁護士、薬剤師など資格志向が一段と強まっています。

plunge into an economic ice age. Luckily in 1996, conditions improved to a certain extent. The improving conditions were greeted with expressions like "The sun has shone" and "The snow is about to melt."

The following year, 1997, was the first year of the abolition of the *shushoku kyotei*, an employment agreement amongst major Japanese corporations, which coordinated and synchronized their recruitment activities. Companies brought forward their recruitment activities and conditions improved overall finally bringing an end to the so-called ice age. But it was just a temporary reprieve and dark clouds began to return in 1998, as Japan slipped back into recession.

Despite this bad climate, male students from top Japanese universities have it pretty easy. It is the female university students who face the most serious difficulties. Even those graduating from leading universities face a much tougher environment than previously. All Japanese companies are attempting to increase the efficiency of their administrative sections and are reducing the number of secretarial and clerical appointments. The Equal Employment Opportunities Law gives women the right to exactly the same work as men, but in reality women are in a much weaker position when it comes to securing employment.

If the recession continues recruitment for women may be plunged back into the ice age again. Woman anticipating this are increasingly focusing on acquiring professional qualifications as doctors, lawyers and pharmacists.

・78

Question　学生に人気のある企業はどこですか？

Answer　就職情報のリクルートリサーチの調査によると、98年に大学を卒業した文系学生の就職志望企業の人気ベスト10は①ソニー　②ＪＴＢ　③全日本空輸　④東京海上火災保険　⑤電通　⑥ＮＴＴドコモ　⑦ＪＲ東日本　⑧日本航空　⑨ＮＨＫ　⑩サントリーの順です。

　理系学生は①ソニー　②スクウェア　③本田技研工業　④キーエンス　⑤マイクロソフト　⑥ＮＴＴドコモ　⑦セガ・エンタープライゼス　⑧Ｐ＆Ｇ　⑨日本ＩＢＭ　⑩マツモトキヨシが上位10社です。

　いずれも一流企業ばかりですが、人気企業にも流行があり、時代によってランキングは結構変わります。

　例えば90年の文系学生の人気企業ベストテンには三菱銀行（現・東京三菱銀行）、三和銀行、住友銀行など銀行が3社も入っていましたが、98年には銀行はベストテンから姿を消しました。不良債権を抱えて経営が苦しい上に、金融不祥事の連続で、銀行のイメージが大幅にダウンしたことが背景にあるようです。

• 78

Q: Which companies are the most popular amongst Japanese students?

A: According to a survey by the employment agency Recruit Research, the ten favorite companies amongst liberal arts university graduates in Japan in 1998 were (1) Sony Corp. (2) Japan Travel Bureau Inc. (3) All Nippon Airways Co., Ltd. (4) The Tokio Marine and Fire Insurance Co., Ltd. (5) Dentsu Inc. (6) NTT Mobile Telecommunications Inc. (7) East Japan Railways Corp. (8) Japan Airlines Co., Ltd. (JAL) (9) NHK (10) Suntory Ltd.

The top ten amongst science and engineering graduates were (1) Sony Corp. (2) Square Co., Ltd. (3) Honda Motor Co., Ltd. (4) Keyence Corp. (5) Microsoft Co., Ltd. (6) NTT Mobile Telecommunications Inc. (7) Sega Enterprises, Ltd. (8) Proctor and Gamble (P&G) (9) IBM Japan Co., Ltd. (10) Matsumotokiyoshi Co., Ltd.

They are all first class companies. However, there are distinct trends in the popularity of companies and these change considerably with the times.

For example, in 1990 the list of top ten companies amongst liberal arts students contained three banks, Mitsubishi Bank (now the Bank of Tokyo-Mitsubishi Ltd.), Sanwa Bank and Sumitomo Bank. By 1998 all these banks had disappeared from the list. Difficult business conditions brought on bad debts and continuous scandals have seriously damaged the banks' images.

90年には商社も三井物産が3位とベストスリーに入っていましたが、三井物産は98年には14位に転落、商社もこのところ人気は落ちています。

一方、ソニーの人気は相変わらずです。時代の先端を行くグローバル企業で、業績も好調なことが人気の秘密のようです。業績はそれほどいいとは言えないのですが、ＪＲ東日本、全日本空輸、日本航空の運輸3社も堅調な人気を保っています。

• 79

Question　日本で「ＭＢＡ」は役に立ちますか？

Answer　東大の蓮見重彦総長は、98年度入学の新入生への言葉の中で、日本の企業や役所の幹部は学歴が低いので、将来を担う若者は学部で研究生活を終えるのではなく、ぜひ大学院に進むよう薦めました。

アメリカの政府高官や企業幹部には修士課程修了者が大勢います。国連など国際機関の採用条件も「修士以上」というところが多いのですが、日本の政府や企業では特に文系の場合、修士という資格は出世にはまったく役に立ちません。むしろ年齢が高い分だけ就職の際、不利になるぐらいです。

In 1990, the trading company Mitsui & Co., Ltd. was in the top three at number three but in 1998 it had dropped to 14th place. Recently, the popularity of trading companies has been falling steadily.

On the other hand, the popularity of Sony Corp. has not changed at all. The secret to its success seems to be that it is a leading global company which consistently performs well. However, the transport companies East Japan Railways Corp., ANA and JAL have managed to hold on to their popularity, despite not achieving particularly good corporate results.

• 79

Q: Are MBAs useful in Japan?

A: At the 1998 entrance ceremony for new students at the University of Tokyo the president of the university, Shigehiko Hasumi, said executives at Japanese companies and public offices had limited education and that young people who wanted to be the torch bearers of the future should not end their research activities at undergraduate level, but should proceed on to graduate school.

Numerous business executives and high ranking government officials in the United States have master degrees. There are a large number of international institutions, like the United Nations, which require at least a master's degree before employment is even considered. But for companies and government officials in Japan, master degrees, especially in the arts, have no effect on promotion prospects. If anything,

　専門知識を持った修士が逆に不利になるのはなぜでしょうか。極端に言うと、日本の企業は学生に対し専門知識は一切求めないからです。

　文系の場合、ある水準以上の大学を卒業していれば、企業は成績よりむしろ仕事に対する意欲や指導力、見識、協調性などを重視するのです。そして社内研修や実際の仕事を通じて新入社員をビジネスマンに育てていくのです。その際、専門知識はまったく無視されるのがオチです。

　ですから、アメリカでは企業幹部へのパスポートとなるハーバードなど一流校のMBAも、日本の企業に就職する限り出世には無意味です。このためせっかく苦労してアメリカの一流校のMBAを取ったのに、社内で評価されずに嘆いているサラリーマンも少なくありません。MBAを活用したければ外資系企業にいくしかありません。

　ただ、理系は別で、企業は学部卒よりも修士課程修了者を優遇しており、工学部などでは多くの学生が大学院に進学しています。

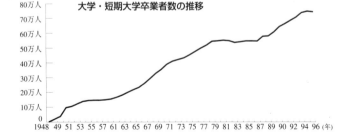

大学・短期大学卒業者数の推移

when it come to recruitment, being older counts against you.

So why is it that having specialist knowledge or a master degree can count against you? To put it bluntly, Japanese companies do not want students with specialist knowledge.

As far as the liberal arts are concerned, if one graduates from a good university above a certain level, the companies put more emphasis on things like enthusiasm, leadership, judgment and cooperativeness than academic results. They develop new recruits into businessmen through real work and internal training schemes. As a result, specialist knowledge is completely ignored.

So unlike the United States, where an MBA from a top university like Harvard is a passport to the boardroom, in Japanese companies having an MBA is irrelevant, when it comes to recruitment or promotion. This is the bane of many *salarymen*, who have worked hard to get MBAs from top schools in the United States, and have subsequently found that their qualifications are not highly prized within the company. If one wants to take advantage of an MBA, the only route is to join a foreign company.

However, the sciences are different. Companies give postdoctoral fellows better treatment than straight graduates and in disciplines such as engineering most students go on to graduate school.

• 80

Question | 役所の「キャリア」と「ノンキャリア」の違いは？

Answer | 国家公務員の採用I種試験に合格して採用された役人は、俗に「キャリア」、II種とIII種合格者は「ノンキャリア」と呼ばれます。キャリアとノンキャリアの昇進スピードの差は、ノンキャリアを各駅停車とするとキャリアは特急ぐらいの違いがあります。

最高到達ポストにも歴然とした違いがあり、キャリアの場合、最低でも本省の課長、出世頭は事務次官になれます。それに比べノンキャリアは、ごくまれに出世頭が本省の末席課長につくことができますが、ほとんどは課長補佐級のポストで役人生活を終えます。

課長補佐というのは、キャリアなら30歳そこそこで全員がつくポスト。キャリアなら10年もかからないでつくポストに、多くのノンキャリアは50代でようやくたどりつくわけです。

キャリアの多くは、東大や京大など一流大学の出身者です。毎年の採用数は全省庁で700

• **80**

Q: What is the difference between career and non-career bureaucrats?

A: Government officials in Japan who pass the grade 1 employment examination are called career (fast track) bureaucrats and those who pass the grade 2 and grade 3 employment examinations are called non-career bureaucrats. The difference in the speed of career advancement between career and non-career bureaucrats is similar to a local train, which stops at every station, and an express train which rushes through to its destination.

The final positions they climb to in their careers as bureaucrats are enormously different. Career bureaucrats will at the very least become departmental directors at the ministries they belong to and the pinnacle of their potential advancement is reaching permanent vice-minister. In comparison the pinnacle for non-career bureaucrats, on rare occasions, is a low level department director. But they are more likely to end their careers as assistants to departmental directors.

The position of assistant to a departmental director is something that most career bureaucrats will have achieved by the time they are 30. It takes almost the whole working life of a non-career bureaucrat finally to reach the position in their 50s, which career bureaucrats normally get to within the first ten years of employment.

Most career bureaucrats are graduates from top Japanese universities such as Tokyo and Kyoto university. Every year

人程度、大蔵省など大きな省でも20人前後と少数精鋭で、政府全体でも2万人強に過ぎません。この少数のキャリアが約83万人の国家公務員の上に君臨するわけです。

キャリアとノンキャリアでは退職後の待遇も違い、キャリアはほぼ全員が天下りを保証されますが、ノンキャリアに保証はありません。以前はキャリアは大卒、ノンキャリアは高校か、短大卒という学歴の差もあったのですが、最近はノンキャリアも大卒者が多くなり、差別待遇に対するノンキャリアの不満は年々強くなっています。

• 81

Question 「東大法卒」は万能ですか？

Answer 教授陣や研究施設、入学難易度などからみて、日本に約600校ある大学の頂点に立つのが東京大学。その東大でも法学部は別格で、エリート中のエリートとみなされています。OBは法曹界はもちろん、政界や官界、一流企業のト

all the ministries combined employ about 700 career bureaucrats. Large ministries like the Ministry of Finance employ very few, less than 20 career bureaucrats each year; while the government as a whole recruits about 20,000 people. This minority of career bureaucrats reign over a total of about 830,000 government officials.

The treatment of career and non-career bureaucrats following retirement is also very different. Career bureaucrats are almost all guaranteed *ama-kudari* (senior post-retirement jobs in the private sector literally meaning descent from heaven). Similar guarantees, however, do not exist for non-career bureaucrats. Previously, career bureaucrats and non-career bureaucrats had distinct academic backgrounds, with career bureaucrats being university educated and non-career bureaucrats being graduates from high schools or two year universities. However, recently the number of university educated non-career bureaucrats has been increasing and dissatisfaction amongst non-career bureaucrats about discriminatory treatment is growing every year.

• 81

Q: Are graduates from the University of Tokyo's law department omnipotent?

A: In terms of the professors, the research facilities and the difficulty in getting in, the University of Tokyo stands at the head of Japan's approximately 600 universities. The law department is special even within the University of Tokyo, as it is seen as the elite amongst the elite. Alumni occupy impor-

ップなど日本のエスタブリッシュメントの中で大きな地位を占めています。

　東洋経済新報社の調査によると、上場企業の社長、役員は東大出身が断トツで、社長は約7人に1人が東大卒です。大蔵省や外務省など中央省庁の事務次官もほとんどが東大、しかも法学部出身者です。

　こうした実績があるため、就職は圧倒的に有利で、法学部の毎年600人から700人の卒業生のほとんどは、官庁や一流企業に就職しています。学生が就職活動で企業を訪問する場合も、人事担当者の応対から違ってきます。一般大学の学生だと課長や一般社員が応対するのが、東大法学部の学生だと部長が応対するといった具合です。

　ただ、最近は採用の際、出身大学よりも人物本位で選考する会社も増えています。受験勉強の成功者である東大法卒業者が企業でも仕事がバリバリできるかというと、必ずしもそうとは限りません。エリート意識が強すぎて周囲と協調できず、社内で浮き上がってしまい、結局、出世できずにサラリーマン生活を終える東大法卒もいます。

tant positions within the Japanese establishment in the judicial, political and bureaucratic worlds and at the top of leading Japanese companies.

According to a survey by the publisher Toyo Keizai Inc. a large number of former students are directors and presidents of public companies. Roughly one in seven presidents of Japanese public corporations is a graduate of the University of Tokyo. Most of the permanent vice-ministers (the highest rank for civil servants in Japan) at the Ministry of Finance, Ministry of Foreign Affairs and other central government ministries are graduates from the University of Tokyo, mostly from the law department.

Due to this track record recruitment prospects for former graduates are overwhelmingly advantageous. The majority of the 600 to 700 people who graduate from the University's law department every year get positions at government offices or at leading companies. When these students look for jobs and visit personnel officers at companies, they receive special treatment. Students from standard universities are usually received by section heads at companies but students at the University of Tokyo and its law department are sometimes greeted by departmental directors.

Recently, however, the number of companies making recruitment decisions based on the individuals themselves and not the name of the university which they come from is on the rise. Graduates from the University of Tokyo's law department who have succeeded in passing a string of examinations do not always make brilliant workers in companies. They can be too acutely aware of their eliteness and unable to cooperate with those around them. Many graduates float up within the company but end their careers as

　就職の際と入社後しばらくは「東大法」は威光を発揮しますが、その後は実力の世界、出世できるかどうかは本人の努力次第で、決して万能ではありません。

• **82**

Question | **日本の労働組合の形態と組織率は?**

Answer | 日本では企業または事業所ごとに組織する企業別組合が圧倒的に多く、全体の90%以上を占めています。労働組合の委員長は出世コースという企業もあります。職業別組合や産業別組合はあまり普及していません。

　組織率は低下傾向にあり、労働者の組合離れが進行しています。中期的にみると雇用者は増えているにもかかわらず、労働組合員は全国で1200万人程度とあまり変わりません。結果的に組織率は下がり、現在は23%程度です。

　組織率は産業別にばらつきがあり、公務員は60%を超えていますが、サービス業などは14%程度、製造業は29%程度です。

　企業別組合は、その上部団体である単位産

salaryman without reaching the very top.

When it comes to recruitment and joining new companies being a graduate of the law department of the University of Tokyo gives one a certain power and authority. But later, it all comes down to personal ability. Promotion really depends on the efforts of the individual, and graduates from the law department at the University of Tokyo are by no mean omnipotent.

• **82**

Q: What is the structure and size of labor unions in Japan?

A: In Japan there is an overwhelmingly large number of independent unions at individual corporations and offices. They represent about 90 percent of all unions in Japan. Industry wide or profession based unions are not widespread.

The overall trend is a decrease in union membership as workers continue to leave unions. If one looks at the medium term trend, despite the fact that the number of people working is increasing, the numbers of union members throughout Japan has hardly changed at all, remaining at around 12 million. This has resulted in a decrease in the rate of membership which is currently about 23 percent of the workforce.

Patterns of union membership differ across industries. Membership by civil servants is above 60 percent but in the service industries membership is only about 14 percent and in manufacturing it is around 29 percent.

The unions at different companies come under the umbrella

業別労働組合連合会（いわゆる「単産」）の支配下に入ります。大きな単産としては自動車産業の自動車総連や電力の電力総連、鉄鋼の鉄鋼労連、電機の電機連合などがあります。

こうした単産の上に全国的な中央組織として連合（日本労働組合総連合会）、金属労協（IMF・JC＝全日本金属産業労働組合協議会）、全労連（全国労働組合総連合）、全労協（全国労働組合連絡協議会）の4団体があります。

この中で最も大きいのは連合で、傘下の組合員数も780万人に達しています。組織票をバックに政治力もあり、国会にも多くの議員を送り込んでいます。

• 83

Question　「フリーター」は新しい職業形態ですか？

Answer　高校や大学、専門学校を卒業しても定職につかず、アルバイトを続ける「フリーター」は少しずつ増えています。本格的に社会に出る前の一種の「猶予期間」のようなもので、職業形態というよりは、生き方のスタイルとい

of governing bodies called Industrial Unions Federations (or *tansan* for short). Large *tansan* include the automobile manufacturing industry's Confederation of Japan Automobile Workers' Unions, the electrical power generating industry's Confederation of Electric Power-Related Industry Workers' Unions of Japan, the steel industry's Japan Federation of Steel Workers, and the electronics manufacturing industry's Japanese Federation of Electrical Machine Workers' Unions.

Above these *tansan* are four central organizations, the Japan Trade Union Confederation (JTUC, Rengo), the International Metal Workers' Federation Japan Council (IMF-JC), the National Confederation of Trade Unions (Zenroren), and the National Trade Union Council (Zenrokyo).

Rengo is the largest amongst the four and has beneath it associated unions whose members number collectively around 7,800,000. It is politically influential due to its ability to mobilize the voting power of its members in government elections and has "dispatched" many people to the national parliament as assemblymen.

• 83

Q: Are *furita*, part-timers, a new style of employee in Japan?

A: The number of people who continue to work part-time even after graduating from high school, university or college and choose not to take up full-time permanent employment is gradually increasing. They are known as *furita*. It is probably more accurate to describe this so-called "stay of

う方が正確でしょう。

　女性の場合、花嫁修業という名目で就職せずに「家事手伝い」（通称『カジテツ』）と称してお花やお茶、料理を習う人は以前からいましたが、最近は、会社などの組織に縛られるよりアルバイトで気ままに暮らしたいという男性のカジテツやフリーターも増えています。

　アルバイトでも日当7000円から1万円ほどもらえ、月に20日も働けば何とか暮らせるからなのでしょうか。なかにはフリーターをしながらカメラマンや作家など憧れの職業を目指す人もいます。資格を取るため勉強する人や、ボランティア活動に精を出したり、海外旅行を続ける人もいます。

　派遣社員もフリーターの一種といえます。一度就職したが仕事がつまらない、職場の人間関係がうまくいかない、などの理由で会社を辞め、定職につかずに派遣会社に登録、いろいろな会社を転々として暮らしているからです。

　大学を卒業してそのまま派遣社員になる「新卒派遣」を選択する女性も増えています。希望の職種が見つからない場合、いろんな会社を経験して自信をつけてから就職しても遅くない、という考えからのようです。

execution" before entering the corporate world as a life style choice, rather than to a new form of employment.

Women choosing not to seek full-time permanent employment have done *hanayome shugyo* (meaning marriage training) by doing *kaji-tetsudai* (helping out with housework) or *kajitetsu* for short. For a long time there have been women who have practised flower arranging, the Japanese tea ceremony and cooking in preparation for getting married. But recently the number of men who choose not to be bound to companies or organizations and prefer to continue working part-time as *kajitetsu* or *furita* is on the increase.

Part-timers can earn from 7,000 yen to 10,000 yen per day and if they manage to work 20 days a month they can eke out a reasonable existence. Included amongst *furita* are people with their sights set on dream jobs such as photographers or writers, people who are studying for professional qualifications and others who do voluntary work or want to travel regularly overseas.

People working for employment agencies are another type of *furita*. They have normally previously had permanent full-time jobs but have given them up because they found their jobs boring or they had some type of trouble at work. They sign on at employment agencies, moving from one job to another without looking for permanent positions.

The number of women who sign on at employment agencies directly after graduating from university is also on the increase. This allows people who cannot find the type of job they are looking for to try out various different jobs at different companies. Once they have gained confidence and experience they often look for full-time permanent positions.

「根付くか、企業のインターンシップ制度」

大学在学中に専攻と関係の深い企業で働くと、大学の単位として認められる学生の就業体験制度「インターンシップ」を導入する企業が、日本でも増えています。

アメリカでは普及しており、日本でも理工系分野では一部導入されていましたが、最近は徐々に文系分野にも広がっています。富士ゼロックスやマイクロソフトなど外資系企業が先鞭を付け、旭化成工業や日本債券信用銀行なども導入を始めました。

98年2月に日本の銀行として初めて実施した日債銀の場合、1週間の体験入社で、デリバティブや金融業務に関する講習、ビジネス文書のまとめ方、会社の信用度の審査方法などの研修を実施しました。

しかし、学生を送り出す大学側の態勢づくりは遅れており、大学の単位として認められないケースがほとんどです。そのため大学を通さず、企業がホームページなどを通じて直接学生を募集する例が大半です。

政府は、制度推進のため大学と企業が運用のルールを作るよう求めていますが、日本にこの制度が定着するかどうかはまだわかりません。

Will company internship programs take root?

The number of companies in Japan introducing internship programs which give students the chance to get work experience, while gaining credits for course work, at companies with businesses related to their field of study is increasing.

In the United States these types of programs are common. In Japan in the areas of science and technology, some companies have introduced programs but recently the number of internship programs for liberal arts students has started to rise. Non-Japanese companies based in Japan like Fuji Xerox Co., Ltd. and Microsoft Corp. have taken the initiative. But other companies like Asahi Chemical Industry Co., Ltd. and the Nippon Credit Bank Ltd. have followed suit, by beginning to introduce their own programs.

In February 1998, the Nippon Credit Bank Ltd. became the first Japanese bank to launch a scheme allowing participants to experience a week's work at the bank. It included special courses on derivatives and financial management, in addition to training on how to write business letters and how to check the credit worthiness of a company.

Universities which can send students on these programs have been slow in making arrangements and most do not officially recognize them nor award students with credits. This has caused many companies to try to recruit students directly for these programs through their company homepages instead of going through the universities.

In an effort to promote internship programs the Japanese government is trying to put together university-industry cooperation rules but it is still too early to say if this system will become established in Japan.

日本の経営者

Management and Ownership in Japan

• 84

Question | 日本で名経営者と言われる人は誰ですか？

Answer | ある新聞社が主要企業の経営者100人に尊敬する経営者を聞いたことがあります。多くの経営者が挙げたのは京セラの稲盛和夫名誉会長、元経団連会長の土光敏夫氏、松下電器産業創業者の松下幸之助氏、本田技研工業の創業者の本田宗一郎氏らでした。健在なのは稲盛氏ただ一人、後の3人はいずれも故人です。

稲盛氏は、京セラをICパッケージの最大手メーカーに育てあげた後、NTTに対抗してDDIを設立、成功しました。成功した後は社長のポストにしがみつくことなく、名誉会長として経営の第一線から身を退き、剃髪して仏門に入りました。独特の経営手法と宗教観、地位にこだわらない潔さが、共感を呼んでいるようです。

松下幸之助氏は小学校しか出ていませんが、奥さんと義弟とわずか3人で始めた町工場の松下電器を、一代で世界有数の家電メーカーに育て上げた人物です。89年に94歳でなくなりましたが、現役時代は「ジャパニーズ・ドリ

• 84

Q: Who are Japan's most famous business executives?

A: A Japanese newspaper which polled a hundred business executives at leading companies in Japan about which business executives they had the most respect for found that Kazuo Inamori, honorary chairman of Kyocera Corp., Toshio Doko, the former chairman of Keidanren, Konosuke Matsushita, the founder of Matsushita Electric Industrial Co., Ltd., and Soichiro Honda, the founder of Honda Motors Co., Ltd. were the most respected. Amongst them only Kazuo Inamori is still alive.

Inamori built Kyocera into the world's largest IC package manufacturer. After this he set up DDI Corp., a telecommunications company which competes successfully with NTT, Japan's largest telecommunications company. Following this success he did not cling to his post but took the position of honorary chairman and retreated from the front line. He then shaved his head and became a Buddhist monk. His unique management techniques, religious beliefs and his graceful unconcern about position struck a chord with business executives.

Konosuke Matsushita only graduated from primary school but with just three people, his wife, brother-in-law and himself started a village factory which he built in one generation, into one of the world's leading household electrical goods manufacturers. He died in 1989, aged 94. He is respected today as

ーム」の体現者として国民的な人気を集めました。91年に84歳でなくなった本田宗一郎氏も町工場を「世界のホンダ」に育て上げた伝説的な人物です。

　土光氏は、石川島播磨重工業社長から財界総理といわれる経団連会長に上り詰めた人ですが、「社会は豊かに、個人は質素に」がモットー。日本ではごく庶民的な食べ物である乾し小魚の「メザシ」が好物で、「メザシの土光さん」と親しまれ、晩年は政府の臨時行政調査会会長として行政改革に取り組み、88年に91歳でなくなりました。

・85

Question **日本にビル・ゲイツのような経営者はいますか？**

Answer ゲイツ氏によく喩えられる「ジャパニーズ・ドリーム」の体現者は、1957年8月生まれの若き経営者、コンピューターソフト卸のソフトバンクの孫正義社長です。

　日本の高校を中退、アメリカの高校を経てカリフォルニア大バークレー校在学中の19歳のときに音声翻訳機を開発、その特許を売って1億円を手にしてアメリカで会社を設立しました。

the embodiment of the "Japanese dream" and is still extremely popular. Soichiro Honda who died in 1991, aged 84, is also a legendary figure for building a local village factory into Honda, a global company.

Toshio Doko who moved from president of Ishikawajima Harima Heavy Industries Co., Ltd. to become the chairman of Keidanren, the Federation of Japanese Economic organizations, a position which is also dubbed the prime minister of Japanese industry, was the force behind the phrase "A plentiful society and a modest individual." He was famous for liking *mezashi*, small dried sardines, an unpretentious common dish in Japan. He was affectionately referred to as Mr Mezashi Doko. In his final years he became involved in government structural reform by becoming chairman of the emergency committee on government reform. He died in 1988, aged 91.

• 85

Q: Is there a "Bill Gates" in Japan?

A: The man most often compared to Gates in Japan, who is also said to be the embodiment of the "Japanese dream" is the young entrepreneur Masayoshi Son, born in 1957. He is the so-called computer software king of Japan and the president of Softbank Corp.

He dropped out of high school in Japan and after attending high school in the United States, studied at the University of California at Berkeley. While still a student aged 19, he developed an audio translating machine. He sold the patent for it for 100 million yen and set up a company in the United States.

　80年にその会社を売却して帰国、81年に日本ソフトバンク（その後ソフトバンクに社名変更）を設立しました。当初、社員はわずか2人。2人の社員を相手に孫氏は、数年後には売上高は数百億円になるとぶち上げました。あきれた2人の社員はすぐに辞めましたが、孫氏の計画は実現しました。

　94年には株式を公開、それを機に大型買収作戦に打って出ます。アメリカのコンピューター関連出版のジフ・デービスを2100億円で、パソコン見本市を展開しているコムデックスを800億円でそれぞれ買収、「平成の買収王」の異名を取ったほどです。社債や転換社債を発行して資本市場から買収資金を調達する手法は「孫流錬金術」と言われました。

　ソフトバンクは98年には東証1部に上場、いまや年間売上高は2000億円を超え、グループ全体で約7000人の社員を抱える企業に成長しました。孫氏はゲイツ氏を「人類史上でキリスト以来の偉人」と尊敬しているそうです。

• **86**

Question｜**日本の代表的な国際派経営者は誰ですか？**

Answer｜最近の注目株は、ソニーの出井伸之社長とトヨタ自動車の奥田碩社長です。

In 1980 that company was bought out and he returned to Japan. In 1981, he set up Softbank Corp. Initially it only had two employees. Son promised the two employees that the company would have a turnover of hundreds of millions of yen within a few years but they got fed up with waiting and quit. Son, however, made his plan a reality.

In 1994 he took the company public, and used the opportunity to launch a big acquisition campaign. He bought a string of companies including the computer magazine publisher, Ziff Davis, in the United States, for 210 billion yen and the computer exhibition organizer, Comdex, for 80 billion yen. He was named the Heisei M&A (merger and acquisition) king. He sold corporate debentures and convertible bonds to tap the world's capital markets for funds for these acquisitions, a method sometimes described in Japan as financial alchemy.

In 1998 Softbank floated part of its stock on the Tokyo Stock Market and its annual turnover has now surpassed 200 billion yen. Softbank has grown into a company with 7,000 employees. Son apparently respects Gates as "the greatest man since Jesus Christ."

• 86

Q: Who are Japan's most renowned international managers?

A: Recently the presidents of Sony Corp. and Toyota Motor Corp., Nobuyuki Idei and Hiroshi Okuda, have been receiving a lot of attention.

　奥田氏は95年8月、28年ぶりに豊田家以外からトヨタの社長に就任しました。慎重で決定に時間がかかるトヨタの経営に「スピード」を持ち込み、即断即決で機動的、攻撃的な企業に変えたと評判です。

「スピードの時代。スピードと知恵の勝負だ。性急といわれるぐらいに早くやる」が奥田氏のモットー。アメリカの経済誌が選んだ世界の最優秀経営者25人に入ったこともあります。

　日本の大企業は、トップがアイデアを出してグイグイ会社を引っ張っていくというより、下から上がってきたアイデアや戦略をトップが採用、決定するというところが大多数です。トップの個性が経営にあまり反映されないので、経営者の顔が見えないとよくいわれます。

　その点、出井氏も奥田氏とともに日本では珍しい「顔の見える経営者」です。ソニーは、デジタル化時代のフロントランナーとしてテレビやビデオだけでなく、ハードとソフトの融合を狙っています。目標達成のため、経営陣の合理化や衛星放送への参入など、社長就任以来、国内、海外で次々に思い切った経営戦略を打ち出しています。

　本田技研工業の川本信彦相談役（前社長）や三菱商事の槙原稔会長、富士ゼロックスの小林陽太郎会長らも国際派の経営者として知られています。

In August 1995, Okuda became the first person outside the Toyoda family in 28 years to become president of Toyota. He is respected for instilling speed to Toyota's management and transforming Toyota, after careful consideration, into a fast moving, mobile, aggressive organization.

"In the era of speed, intelligence and speed brings victory," is his motto. Okuda's speed, which is said to border on impatience, is one of the reasons why he was chosen by an American financial newspaper as one of the world's top 25 excellent managers.

At Japan's major corporations top managers normally adopt ideas and strategies that come up through the ranks, as opposed to creating their own ideas and vigorously leading the company forwards. The personalities of the top managers are not usually reflected in management itself, which has led to Japanese companies being described as faceless.

In this respect, Idei and Okuda are rare, as they are highly visible managers. Sony Corp. is a front runner in the digital age, not just with its televisions and videos but with its plan of fusing together hardware and software. In order to achieve this objective its management has been rationalized and the company has started to participate in satellite broadcasting, since Idei became president. A series of bold domestic and overseas business strategies has also been launched.

In addition, the former president of Honda Motor Corp., Nubuhiko Kawamoto; the chairman of Mitsubishi Corp, Minoru Makihara; and the chairman of Fuji Xerox Co., Ltd., Yotaro Kobayashi, are renown as internationally-minded managers.

• 87

Question　**財界活動の目的と実態は？**

Answer　日本には主な経済団体として経済団体連合会（経団連）、日本経営者団体連盟（日経連）、日本商工会議所（日商）、経済同友会の4つがあり、経済4団体と呼ばれています。企業トップの財界活動は主にこの4団体を舞台にしています。

　最も大きな影響力を持っているのは、日本の有力企業が加入している経団連で、財界の総本山と呼ばれており、トップの会長は「財界総理」として日本の経営者の頂点に立っています。

　企業経営者の声を代弁して政府の政策に注文をつけるのが最大の役割で、政界に影響力を及ぼすため、政治献金の窓口にもなっています。外国の経済団体との交流なども行っています。

　日経連は、労働組合の活動に対し経営権を守るために設立された団体で、毎年の春闘についての対応方針を策定するなど労働問題に特化しているため、「財界労務部」ともいわれています。

• 87

Q: What do Japan's finance and business organizations do?

A: The major finance and business organizations in Japan are Keidanren, the Federation of Economic Organizations; Nikkeiren, the Japan Federation of Employers; Nissho, the Japan Chamber of Commerce and Industry; and Keizai-doyukai, the Japan Committee of Economic Development. They are often referred to collectively as *Keizai-yon-dantai*, the four economic organizations.

The most influential organization, which has most major Japanese corporations as members, is Keidanren, the Federation of Economic Organizations. It is referred to as the high church of the world of business. The chairman of this top organization is considered the prime minister of the business world standing at the summit of Japanese management.

His most important role is to be the representative voice of Japanese business and speak out on government policy. In order to enhance the clout and influence of the business world the organization is a liaison center for political donations. It also conducts exchanges with economic and business organizations overseas.

Nikkeiren, the Japan Federation of Employers was set up as an organization to protect the interests of companies against labor union activities. Every year at the *shunto* (the spring labor offensive) it formulates responses to wage demands and specializes in labor disputes. It is often called

　日商は全国各地の商工会議所の連合体で、加盟企業は約160万社にも達しますが、加盟しているのは主に中小企業。中小企業の声を代弁する団体とみられています。

　経済同友会は大企業の役員が個人の資格で参加、さまざまなテーマについて研究したり、発表したりする場です。

• 88

Question | 経団連会長はどうやって選ばれるのですか？

Answer | 経団連は98年5月末の総会で、豊田章一郎・トヨタ自動車会長の退任と、今井敬副会長（新日本製鉄会長）の会長昇格、副会長10人の就任を決めました。

「歴代の経団連会長」		
		出身企業など
1948年―56年	石川一郎	日産化学工業
56年―68年	石坂泰三	第一生命、東芝
68年―74年	植村甲午郎	官僚
74年―80年	土光敏夫	東芝
80年―86年	稲山嘉寛	新日本製鉄
86年―90年	斎藤英四郎	新日本製鉄
90年―94年	平岩外四	東京電力
94年―98年	豊田章一郎	トヨタ自動車
98年―	今井敬	新日本製鉄

the labor relations office of the business world.

Nissho, the Japan Chamber of Commerce and Industry, is the coordination center for all the chamber of commerce and industry offices throughout Japan. It has about 1,600,000 member companies. Its members consist mostly of small and medium sized companies and it acts as their voice of representation.

Keizai-doyukai, the Japan Committee of Economic Development is an organization which company directors belong to as individuals. It conducts various kinds of business related research and regularly publishes reports.

• 88

Q: How is the head of Keidanren chosen?

A: Keidanren, the Federation of Economic Organizations (Japan's most powerful federation of business leaders), decided at its annual general meeting at the end of May 1998, to promote its vice chairman Takashi Imai (chairman of Nippon Steel Corp.) to chairman, taking over from retiring chairman Shoichiro Toyoda (chairman of Toyota Motor Corp.). It also approved the appointment of 10 deputy chairmen.

経済4団体の概要

名 称	略 称	設立年	会 員	代 表 者
経済団体連合会	経団連	1946年	企業、団体など1251	会長・今井敬
日本経営者団体連盟	日経連	1948年	105団体	会長・根本二郎
日本商工会議所	日商	1922年	全国各地の517商工会議所	会頭・稲葉興作
経済同友会	同友会	1946年	経営者ら約1600人	代表幹事・牛尾治朗

今井会長は、戦後の経団連創立以来9代目の会長で、6代目会長の斎藤英四郎氏以来久々の鉄鋼業界出身者となりました。会長の任期は2年ですが、通常は2期4年務めます。

豊田氏が退任の意向を示唆して以来、後継の会長人事は何かと話題になりました。新会長は人格、識見や説得力、年齢などを考慮して副会長の中から会長が指名するのが恒例です。今回、候補者に挙げられたのは今井氏と関本忠弘副会長（NEC会長）でした。

今井氏は合理主義者、理論派として知られています。よく勉強し、よく働きます。政府に対してもずけずけと発言しますが、「頭が良すぎるのが欠点」との指摘もあります。

一方の関本氏は、東大の物理学科出身の技術者で人格は円満、日本の産業界をリードするコンピューター業界出身者でもあり、資格は十分。どちらも甲乙つけがたく、豊田会長も人選には相当頭を悩ませたようですが、最終的に若い今井氏を指名しました。

副会長は各業界や企業グループの代表者から選ばれます。今度の総会を機に12人から10人に減り、退任したさくら銀行の末松謙一相談役に代わる銀行界出身者は選ばれませんでした。銀行界の地盤沈下を象徴するかのような人事でした。

Imai becomes the 9th chairman of Keidanren since it was set up after the Second World War. He is the first chairman for some time, in fact the first since the sixth chairman, Eishiro Saito, to come from the steel industry. The appointment is for two years but generally the position is held for two terms for a total of 4 years.

After Toyoda indicated his intention to retire, choosing his successor became a bit of a problem. It is customary for the new chairman to be chosen from amongst the vice chairmen taking into consideration personality, opinions, persuasiveness and age. This time there were two candidates, Takashi Imai and Tadahiro Sekimoto, chairman of NEC Corp.

Imai, a pragmatist, is known to be a theorist as well as someone who studies and works hard. He has been a vocal critic of the government but is thought to be a bit "too clever."

On the other hand, Sekimoto, an engineer who graduated from the physics department of the University of Tokyo is said to have a well integrated personality. Coming from the computer industry, which is currently playing a leading role within Japanese industry, he was well qualified for the job. It was very difficult to differentiate between the two of them and the chairman, Toyoda, struggled over the decision but finally came out in favor of the younger Imai.

The deputy chairmen are chosen from representatives of various industries and business groups. This time at the annual general meeting their number was reduced from 12 to 10. Kenichi Suematsu from Sakura Bank resigned. But he was not replaced with anyone else from the banking world, a decision that seems to highlight the falling influence of banks in Japan.

・**89**

Question｜**日本では世襲経営者が多いですか？**

Answer｜国際的な企業でも創業者一族が経営トップを占める例は多く、世襲制の是非がしばしば話題になります。

　松下電器産業は故・松下幸之助氏が一代で築いた企業ですが、幸之助氏の娘婿の松下正治氏が会長を務め、正治氏の長男の正幸氏は現在、副社長です。

　トヨタ自動車は、豊田佐吉氏が1926年に創業した豊田自動織機製作所という会社の自動車部門として誕生、それが分離して大きくなった会社です。そのため現在の会長の章一郎氏をはじめ豊田家一族が長くトップを務めており、奥田碩氏は28年ぶりに豊田家以外から出た社長です。

　三洋電機も創業者の井植歳男氏の長男、敏氏が会長、敏氏の長男の敏雅氏が取締役を務めています。ダイエーの創業者で会長兼社長の中内㓛氏の長男、潤氏も副社長で、ジャスコの岡田元也社長は岡田卓也会長の長男です。

　世襲制には社の内外から批判があります。松下電器の正幸氏はいずれ社長に就任するとみられていますが、同社の元社長で現在相談

• 89

Q: In Japan are there many business leaders who inherit their positions?

A: In Japan the top executives of multinational companies are often relatives of the founders of the organizations. The rights and wrongs of this hereditary system are hotly debated.

Matsushita Electric Industrial Co., Ltd. was built in one generation by the late Konosuke Matsushita. But Konosuke's son-in-law, Masaharu Matsushita, is now chairman and his son, Masayuki Matsushita, is vice president of the company.

Toyota Motor Corp. was born out of the automobile section of Toyoda Automatic Loom Works founded by Sakichi Toyoda in 1926 from which it split off and grew. The Toyoda family, including the current chairman Shoichiro Toyada, ran the company for a long time. The current president, Hiroshi Okuda, is the first president for 28 years not to come from the Toyoda family.

The oldest son of Toshio Iue, the founder of Sanyo Electric Co., Ltd. Toshi Iue, is chairman of the company and his oldest son, Toshimasa Iue, is a director of the company. Jun Nakauchi, oldest son of Isao Nakauchi, founder, chairman, and president of Daie, Inc., is vice president of the company. Motoya Okada, president of Jusco Co., Ltd., is the son of the chairman, Takuya Okada.

This inheritance system is criticized from both within the companies themselves and outside. Masayuki Matsushita is expected to be appointed president of Matsushita Electric

役の山下俊彦氏は97年夏、「創業者の孫という
だけで社長になるのはおかしい」と世襲制に
警鐘を鳴らしました。

　薬品メーカー、ツムラの創業者の孫で前社
長の津村昭氏のように会社を私物化し、特別
背任罪に問われた例もあります。

　最近、「会社は誰のものか」という「企業統
治論」が問題になっています。企業は社会の
公器、世襲制は企業の私物化につながりかね
ず、好ましいものではないので、社長や役員
の子弟は入社させない決まりの会社もありま
す。

・**90**

Question │ **日本の会社の社訓とはなんですか？**

Answer │ 昔から日本の家庭には家の方針に当たる「家
訓」というものがあります。家訓の会社版が
「社訓」です。会社も家庭と同じように方針、
規律が必要というわけで、経営理念、哲学の
ようなものです。
　松下電器産業の本社では、毎朝始業前に社
員が起立して「産業報国の精神」「感謝報恩の
精神」など巻物に書かれた「遵守すべき精神」

Industrial Co., Ltd. but the former president who now acts as an advisor to the company, Toshihiko Yamashita, stated publicly in the summer of 1997 that it is ridiculous that someone can become president just because he is the grandchild of the founder, sounding the alarm bell.

There are cases like, for example, the former president of the pharmaceutical company Tsumura & Co., Akira Tsumura, the grandson of the founder of the company, who treated the company as his own personal property and ended up being charged with malpractice.

Recently there has been a debate about who companies belong to and who should reign over them. Companies are public institutions and the hereditary system which can lead to companies being treated as personal property is unwelcome. There are in fact companies which prohibit sons and children of presidents and directors from joining the corporation.

• 90

Q: What are *shakun*, the ethical codes of Japanese companies?

A: For a long time Japanese households have had family precepts or codes known as *kakun*. The corporate versions of these are *shakun*. Just like households, companies need codes and regulations such as corporate principles or philosophy.

At the head office of Matsushita Electric Industrial Co., Ltd. every morning before work begins, staff recite the company principles which are written on a scroll. They include

を唱和します。これは創業者である故松下幸之助氏の社長時代からの伝統です。

　幸之助氏の経営哲学は、「生活物資を水のごとく無尽蔵たらしめる」というもので、「水道哲学」ともいわれています。松下電器の社員はこの哲学を学び、実践しなければなりません。毎朝の唱和もその一環です。

　日本の3大企業グループの一つ、住友グループの経営理念は「浮利を追わない」という堅実主義です。「石橋をたたいて渡る」という諺がありますが、住友グループはこの経営理念を守り、他の企業グループから「石橋をたたいても渡らない」と陰口をたたかれるほど慎重な経営で有名です。

　会社だけでなく日本の経営者はみな教訓が好きで、どこの企業のトップも必ず「座右の銘」という好きな格言をよく口にします。『論語』など中国の古典からの引用が多いのですが、丸井の青井忠雄社長の好きな言葉はちょっと現実的で「株は天の声」。

statements on "contribution to society," "fairness and honesty," and "courtesy and humility." This tradition started when Konosuke Matsushita, the founder of the company, was president.

Konosuke's management philosophy was that everyday necessities should be like flowing water—inexhaustible. This was called "the tap philosophy," a theory by which consumers could easily get access to new products in a similar way to water by turning on a tap. Matsushita employees have to learn the principles and practice this philosophy. Reciting them each morning before work is part of this process.

The Sumitomo Group, one of Japan's top three industrial groups, has a management philosophy of "not pursuing frivolous profits." It has a reputation associated with the Japanese phrase, "Sound out the safety of a stone bridge before you cross." The group is famous for its prudent management style and sticks to its principles to such an extent that staff at other industrial groups in Japan criticize Sumitomo for "not even crossing bridges it has tested."

Both Japanese corporations and Japanese business executives have a soft spot for Confucius. Top managers at almost all Japanese companies have a favorite motto or saying that they often use. Many are taken from the Analects (teachings) of Confucius or ancient Chinese proverbs. The president of Marui Co., Ltd., Tadao Aoi, likes the rather pragmatic saying, "Stocks are the voice of heaven."

• 91

Question | 日本の平均的な大企業の社長像は？

Answer | 平均年齢61歳、在任期間は6年から8年程度、趣味はゴルフ、読書、囲碁、出身大学は東大、京大、一橋大、早稲田、慶応の5大学のどれか、既婚でもちろん男性…。大企業の平均的な社長像はこんな感じです。ただしこれはあくまで平均。オーナー社長とサラリーマン社長では大きく異なります。

　サラリーマン社長は早くて50代前半、ふつうは50代後半から60歳前後に社長になり、6年か8年程度社長を務め、60代後半、遅くとも70歳ごろまでには会長に就任するか、相談役などに退くのが一般的なパターンです。

　大企業の場合、役員がポストにしがみついて後進になかなか道を譲らないという「老害」を防ぐため、社員同様、役員にも定年制を設けているところが多いので、いつまでも社長にとどまることはできません。

　しかし、オーナー経営者の場合はまったく

• 91

Q: What is the profile of the average company president in Japan?

A: The average Japanese president is 61 years old. The position of president has probably been held for between 6 and 8 years. The president's hobbies will include golf, reading and playing the traditional game *go*. The average president is usually a graduate of one of the following five Japanese universities: Tokyo, Kyoto, Hitotsubashi, Waseda or Keio. The president will be married and, needless to say, male. This is the typical profile of the average president of a major Japanese corporation. But this is just the average; there is a considerable difference between owner-presidents and *salarymen*-presidents.

Salarymen-presidents will, at the earliest, become president in the first half of their fifties but more usually in their late fifties or early sixties. They will normally serve as president for 6 to 8 years. The usual pattern is that in their late sixties or early seventies they will be appointed chairman or take on the role of company advisor.

In major corporations to stop directors from clinging to posts, making it difficult for junior colleagues to replace them, and in order to avoid ageing problems, many companies have set up fixed retirement systems for directors, similar to those for regular employees so that it is impossible to remain president forever.

However, the situation for owner-managers is completely

違います。サラリーマン役員を飛び越えて30代で社長に就任するケースや、社長在任40年、老害批判もどこ吹く風で、80歳を過ぎてもなお社長のポストに居座る経営者もいます。

オーナーでなくても、会社の「中興の祖」として「死ぬまで社長を辞めない」と公言して社長のポストに何十年もとどまった大手繊維会社の社長もいました。女性社長は非常に少なく、97年現在、上場企業の社長を務める女性はわずか4人です。

・92

Question 日本では社長（頭取）と会長、実権はどちらにありますか？

Answer アメリカの企業ではCEO（最高経営責任者）が実権を持っており、会長を兼務しているケースが多いようですが、日本ではCEO制度は定着しておらず、ほとんどの企業では社長（銀行では頭取）が実権を握っています。

会長制を敷いている企業では、社長を何年か務めた後、会長に就任します。通常、会長に就任する段階で経営の実権は社長に譲り、第一線から退きます。会長になってからはときどき社長にアドバイスする程度で日々の経

different. There are some cases of people in their thirties who are made president over *salarymen* directors, and then there are those over the age of eighty who having been president for forty years still cling to their posts despite rumors of senility.

But this does not only apply to owner-presidents. There was the case of the president of a leading textile company who held onto his post for decades. He treated the company as his own personal realm, publicly declaring that he would not retire until the day he dies.

Few women are presidents of companies. In 1997, there were only 4 women amongst all the presidents of all public companies in Japan.

• 92

Q: Does the real power in Japanese companies rest with the president or chairman of the company?

A: In American companies the real executive power rests with the Chief Executive Officer (CEO) and there are many cases of the position of chairman being held concurrently. In Japan the CEO system is still not well established and in the majority of Japanese companies the real authority rests with the *shacho*, president or in the case of banks *todori*, president.

In companies with the chairmanship system the president will take up the post of chairman after working as president for a number of years. Usually, at the stage when the position of chairman is acquired real management and executive authority is passed over to the president and the indi-

営にはタッチせず、財界活動などに専念する
ケースが多いようです。

　企業によっては社長が国内部門、会長が海
外部門を担当するという具合に、責任を分担
しているところもあります。

　ただ、なかには長い間社長をやり、会長に
なってからも実権を握り続けるケースもあり
ます。そのような企業は、平安時代に天皇の
位を息子などに譲った上皇や法皇が、実権を
握り続けた「院政」になぞらえて、会社の
「院政」と揶揄されます。

　こういう変則的な企業では社長が実権を持
たない傀儡政権になったり、会長と社長が派
閥を作り、人事抗争が起きるところもありま
す。

　まれなケースとして会長を退任した長老が
実権を握り続ける会社もあります。全日本空
輸の若狭得治相談役は、会長から名誉会長に
なっても人事権を手放さず、会社に君臨して
いましたが、人事抗争の末、82歳でようやく
相談役に退きました。

vidual retreats from everyday business activities. After becoming chairman there is very little or no connection with the everyday running of the business and the chairman will only supply the occasional advice to the president. Many company chairmen devote themselves to industry-wide activities.

At some companies the responsibilities are split, giving the president the role of looking after domestic affairs and the chairman, overseas activities.

But there are cases of individuals who have held the position of president for a long time, keeping real authority even after they have become chairman. This is dubbed corporate *insei* in an unfavorable reference to the Heian Period (1192–1333). Then, Japanese emperors passed on their position to their sons but still continued to hold on to the reigns of power in what was known as *insei*.

In these unorthodox companies, where the president does not hold the real power and ends up running a puppet administration, the president and chairman can end up creating factions within the company, which can create personnel conflicts.

In rare cases at some companies the retired chairman can continue to keep a grip on power as a senior figure within the organization. Tokuji Wakasa, advisor at All Nippon Airways Co., Ltd. (ANA) did not let go of his authority over personnel related matters even after he moved from chairman to chairman emeritus and he continued to reign over the corporation. This ended up causing personnel conflicts within ANA and finally at the age of 82 he retreated to his current advisory role at the company.

「企業と政治献金」

日本の政治はカネがかかりすぎるといわれてきました。国会議員の場合、政府が提供する東京の事務所や秘書の他に、地元選挙区にも事務所や私設秘書をおいたり、支持者に対する接待や贈り物などでかなりの出費を余儀なくされます。

かつて自民党の1党支配体制下では、自民党はこうした費用をほとんど企業からの献金で賄っていました。「民主主義を担保し、市場経済を維持するためのコスト」というのが、経済界の大義名分でした。自民党への政治献金の斡旋窓口になっていたのが経団連です。経団連は、自民党から要請された額を各業界、企業に割り振り、この自民党と経済界の癒着の構造が自民党長期政権とともに政治腐敗の原因となっていました。

こうした反省から細川政権時代の1994年に政治改革の一貫として政府による政党助成制度が導入され、国民1人当たり250円、総額309億円の助成金が議員数などに応じて毎年政党に配分されることになりました。自民党1党支配の終了と政党助成の導入をきっかけに経団連は献金斡旋を中止しました。

しかし、経団連を通さない企業献金はまだ続いています。

Corporations and Political Donations

Politics in Japan costs excessive amounts of money. For National Diet (parliament) members in addition to the Tokyo office and secretaries which are provided to them by the state, they set up local constituency offices which need secretaries and funds are also needed for entertaining and buying gifts for supporters. This inevitably takes up a large proportion of their expenses.

Previously, when the Liberal Democratic Party (LDP) dominated Japanese politics and governed Japan under a system of one-party rule, the LDP covered the majority of these expenses through political donations it received from companies. The business world justified this as "the cost for securing democracy and maintaining a market economy."

The Federation of Economic Organizations, Keidanren, acted as an intermediary liaison office for such donations from companies to the LDP. After Keidanren received requests for the amount of funds needed by the LDP for its activities it assigned various industries and companies the job of raising the money. The structure of this cozy relationship between big business and the LDP is one of the reasons the LDP has been able to cling to power for so long and also one of the main causes of political corruption.

A series of scandals related to political donations led the Hosokawa administration in 1994, as part of the political reform process, to introduce new legislation which brought about the introduction of the political fund raising system. This system makes allocations every year to each party depending on the number of members of parliament the party has from a total subsidy of 30.9 billion yen or 250 yen per person in Japan. The end of one-party rule by the LDP and the introduction of the subsidy for political parties led to the cancellation by Keidanren of its function as an intermediary for political donations.

However, political donations from companies not channelled through Keidanren still continue.

英語で話す日本ビジネスQ&A
──ここが知りたい、日本のカイシャ──
Frequently Asked Questions on Corporate Japan

1998年 11 月 13日　第 1 刷発行

著　者　　米山司理
　　　　　リチャード・ネイサン

発行者　　野間佐和子

発行所　　講談社インターナショナル株式会社
　　　　　〒112-8652　東京都文京区音羽 1-17-14
　　　　　電話：03-3944-6493　（編集）
　　　　　　　　03-3944-6492　（営業）

印刷所　　大日本印刷株式会社

製本所　　株式会社　堅省堂

落丁本、乱丁本は、講談社インターナショナル営業部宛にお送りください。送料
小社負担にてお取替えいたします。なお、この本についてのお問い合わせは、
編集局第二出版部宛にお願いいたします。本書の無断複写（コピー）は著作権
法上での例外を除き、禁じられています。

定価はカバーに表示してあります。

Copyright © Yoneyama Morimasa and Richard Nathan
ISBN4-7700-2165-8

対訳 日本事典 (全1巻)

The Kodansha Bilingual Encyclopedia of Japan

講談社インターナショナル 編

B5判（182 x 257 mm）
上製　箱入り
944ページ（カラー口絵16ページ）
ISBN 4-7700-2130-5

**ビジネス、海外駐在、
留学、ホームステイなど、
さまざまな国際交流の場で、
幅広くご活用いただけます。**

特色

**「日本」を国際的な視点で理解できる幅広い知識と、
実用的な英語が身につきます。**

1. 現代の政治制度、最新の経済情報を豊富に記載し、日本を総合的に理解できる。
2. 分野別の構成により、テーマに沿って自然に読み進むことができる。
3. 豊富なイラストと図版を収録し、完全対訳のレイアウトと欄外のキーワードで、重要単語や表現の日英相互参照に便利。
4. 日本国憲法、重要な国際条約、年表をいずれも日英併記で巻末に収録。
5. 英語からも日本語（ローマ字）からも引けるインデックスつき。

内容構成

地理 / 歴史 / 政治 / 経済 / 社会 / 文化 / 生活